Nick Vandome

macOS Sierra

in easy steps

covers macOS version 10.12

In easy steps is an imprint of In Easy Steps Limited
16 Hamilton Terrace · Holly Walk · Leamington Spa
Warwickshire · United Kingdom · CV32 4LY
www.ineasysteps.com

Notice of Liability
Every effort has been made to ensure that this book contains accurate
and current information. However, In Easy Steps Limited and the
author shall not be liable for any loss or damage suffered by readers
as a result of any information contained herein.

Trademarks
OS X® and macOS® are registered trademarks of Apple Computer
Inc. All other trademarks are acknowledged as belonging to their
respective companies.

In Easy Steps Limited supports The Forest Stewardship Council (FSC),
the leading international forest certification organization. All our titles
that are printed on Greenpeace approved FSC certified paper carry the
FSC logo.

MIX
Paper from
responsible sources
FSC® C020837

Printed and bound in the United Kingdom

ISBN 978-1-84078-744-3

33614057812173

Contents

1   **Introducing macOS Sierra**   7

About macOS Sierra   8
Installing macOS Sierra   9
The macOS Environment   10
About Your Mac   12
About System Preferences   16
Search Options   17
Using Siri   18
Searching with Siri   19
Changing the Resolution   22
Accessibility   23
The Spoken Word   25
Shutting Down   26

2   **Getting Up and Running**   27

Introducing the Dock   28
Apps on the Dock   29
Setting Dock Preferences   30
Stacks on the Dock   32
Dock Menus   34
Working with Dock Items   35
Trash   37
System Preferences   38
About iCloud   40
Setting up iCloud   41
About the iCloud Drive   42
Continuity   44
Handoff   45
About Family Sharing   46
Using Family Sharing   48
Desktop Items   52
Ejecting Items   53
Resuming   54

3   **Finder**   55

Working with the Finder   56
Finder Folders   57
Finder Views   59

Covers 62
Quick Look 63
Finder Toolbar 64
Finder Sidebar 65
Finder Search 66
Copying and Moving Items 67
Working with Folders 68
Selecting Items 69
Finder Tabs 70
Tagging in the Finder 72
Spring-loaded Folders 74
Burnable Folders 75
Actions Button 76
Sharing from the Finder 77
Menus 78

4 Navigating in macOS Sierra 79

The macOS Way of Navigating 80
macOS Scroll Bars 81
Split View 82
Trackpad Gestures 84
Magic Mouse Gestures 92
Multi-Touch Preferences 95
Mission Control 97
Spaces 98

5 macOS Sierra Apps 99

Launchpad 100
Full Screen Apps 102
macOS Apps 104
Accessing the App Store 105
Downloading Apps 106
Finding Apps 108
Managing Your Apps 110

6 Getting Productive 111

Contacts (Address Book) 112
Calendar 114
Taking Notes 116
Setting Reminders 118
Notifications 120
Getting Around with Maps 122

Preview 126
Printing 127
macOS Utilities 128
Creating PDF Documents 130

7 Internet and Email 131

Getting Connected 132
Safari 134
Safari Sidebar 135
Safari Tabbed Browsing 136
Safari Top Sites 137
Adding Bookmarks 138
Safari Reader 139
Mail 140
Using Mail 141
Messaging 142
FaceTime 144

8 Digital Lifestyle 145

Using the Photos App 146
Viewing Photos 147
Editing Photos 149
Photo Memories 150
Starting with iTunes 152
Buying Music with iTunes 153
Using Apple Music 154
Reading with iBooks 155

9 Sharing macOS 157

Adding Users 158
Deleting Users 160
Fast User Switching 161
Parental Controls 162

10 Networking 165

Networking Overview 166
Network Settings 168
File Sharing 169
Connecting to a Network 170

11 Maintaining macOS — 173

Time Machine	174
Disk Utility	178
System Information	179
Activity Monitor	180
Updating Software	181
Gatekeeper	182
Privacy	183
Problems with Apps	184
General Troubleshooting	185

Index — 187

1 Introducing macOS Sierra

macOS Sierra is the latest operating system from Apple, for its range of desktop and laptop computers. This chapter introduces macOS Sierra, showing how to install it and get started using its array of features including, for the first time, the digital voice assistant, Siri.

8   About macOS Sierra

9   Installing macOS Sierra

10   The macOS Environment

12   About Your Mac

16   About System Preferences

17   Search Options

18   Using Siri

19   Searching with Siri

22   Changing the Resolution

23   Accessibility

25   The Spoken Word

26   Shutting Down

About macOS Sierra

macOS Sierra is the 12th version (10.12) of the operating system for Apple computers; the iMac, MacBook, Mac Mini and Mac Pro. Although it is still a development of the OS X (pronounced 'ten') operating system for Macs, the naming convention has been changed to macOS, to more clearly identify it as belonging to the Mac, rather than a mobile device such as the iPad or iPhone. Like earlier versions, it is based on the UNIX programming language, which is a very stable and secure operating environment and ensures that macOS is one of the most stable consumer operating systems that has ever been designed. More importantly for the user, it is also one of the most stylish and user-friendly operating systems available.

When one of macOS Sierra's predecessors, OS X Mountain Lion, was introduced in 2012, it contained a range of innovative functions that were inspired by Apple's mobile devices: iPhone, iPad and iPod Touch. This was continued with the next versions of the operating system, OS X Yosemite, OS X El Capitan and now macOS Sierra. The three main areas where the functionality of the mobile devices has been transferred to the desktop and laptop operating system are:

- The way apps can be downloaded and installed. Instead of using a disc, macOS Sierra utilizes the App Store to provide apps, which can be installed in a couple of steps.

- Options for navigating around pages and applications on a trackpad or a Magic Mouse. Instead of having to use a mouse or a traditional laptop trackpad, macOS Sierra continues to use Multi-Touch Gestures for navigating apps and web pages.

- Siri, Apple's digital voice assistant, has now made the transition from being only available on mobile devices to being included with macOS Sierra too.

macOS Sierra continues the evolution of the operating system, by adding more features and enhancing the ones that were already there. These include: enhancements to the Photos app, making it easier to find photos according to people and places, and a Memories function for automatically displaying your best photos; improvements to the iCloud Drive for storing files; a wider range of emojis for adding to Messages; and a redesigned interface for iTunes and Apple Music.

UNIX is an operating system that has traditionally been used for large commercial mainframe computers. It is renowned for its stability and ability to be used within different computing environments.

The New icon pictured above indicates a new or enhanced feature introduced with the latest version of macOS – macOS Sierra.

Installing macOS Sierra

When it comes to installing macOS Sierra you do not need to worry about an installation CD or DVD; it can be downloaded and installed directly from the online App Store. New Macs will have macOS Sierra installed. The following range is compatible with macOS Sierra, and can be upgraded with it:

- iMac (Late 2009 or newer)

- MacBook (Late 2009 or newer)

- MacBook Pro (2010 or newer)

- MacBook Air (2010 or newer)

- Mac Mini (2010 or newer)

- Mac Pro (2010 or newer)

If you want to install macOS Sierra on an existing Mac, you will need to have the minimum requirements of:

- OS X Lion (10.7.5) or later (see first tip).

- Intel Core 2 Duo, Core i3, Core i5, Core i7 or Xeon processor, or higher.

- 2GB of memory and 8.8GB of available storage for installation.

If your Mac meets these requirements, you can download and install macOS Sierra, for free, as follows:

1 Click on this icon on the Dock to access the App Store (or select **Software Update**, see tip)

2 Locate the **macOS Sierra** icon (this will be on the **Featured** page or within the **Utilities** category)

macOS Sierra
Utilities

DOWNLOAD ▼

3 Click on the **Download** button and follow the installation instructions

macOS Sierra is a free upgrade from the App Store if you already have the Lion, Mountain Lion, Mavericks, Yosemite or El Capitan versions of OS X on your Mac.

To check your computer's software version and upgrade options, click on **Apple menu** > **About This Mac** from the main Menu bar. Click on the **Overview** tab and click on the **Software Update** button. See page 13 for details.

The macOS Environment

The first most noticeable element about macOS is its elegant user interface. This has been designed to create a user friendly graphic overlay to the UNIX operating system at the heart of macOS, and it is a combination of rich colors and sharp, original graphics. The main elements that make up the initial macOS environment are:

Apple menu   Menu bar   Windows   Menu bar icons

The Dock   Desktop

Hot tip

The Dock is designed to help make organizing and opening items as quick and easy as possible. For a detailed look at the Dock, see Chapter Two.

Don't forget

Many of the behind-the-scenes features of macOS Sierra are aimed at saving power on your Mac. These include time coalescing technologies for saving processing and battery power; features for saving energy when apps are not being used; power saving features in Safari for ignoring additional content provided by web page plug-ins; and memory compression to make your Mac quicker and more responsive.

The **Apple menu** is standardized throughout macOS, regardless of the app in use.

Menus

Menus in macOS contain commands for the operating system and any relevant apps. If there is an arrow next to a command it means there are subsequent options for the item. Some menus also incorporate the same transparency as the sidebar so that the background shows through.

...cont'd

Transparency

One feature in macOS Sierra is that the sidebar and toolbars in certain apps are transparent so that you can see some of the Desktop behind it. This also helps the uppermost window blend in with the background:

1 In certain apps with a sidebar, such as the Finder or Safari, the background appears behind the sidebar

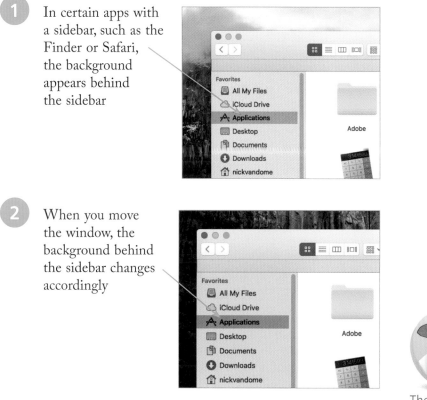

2 When you move the window, the background behind the sidebar changes accordingly

Window buttons

These appear in any open macOS window and can be used to manipulate the window. They include a full screen option. Use the window buttons to, from left to right, close a window, minimize a window or maximize a window.

If an app has full screen functionality, this green button is available:

If an option is gray, it means it is not available, i.e. the screen cannot be maximized.

Don't forget

The red window button is used to close a window and in some cases, such as Notes, Reminders and Calendar, it also closes the app. The amber button is used to minimize a window, so that it appears at the right-hand side of the Dock.

About Your Mac

When you buy a new Mac, you will almost certainly check the technical specifications before you make a purchase. Once you have your Mac, there will be times when you will want to view these specifications again, such as the version of macOS in use, the amount of memory and the amount of storage. This can be done through the About This Mac option, which can be accessed from the Apple menu. To do this:

1 Click on the **Apple menu** and click on the **About This Mac** link

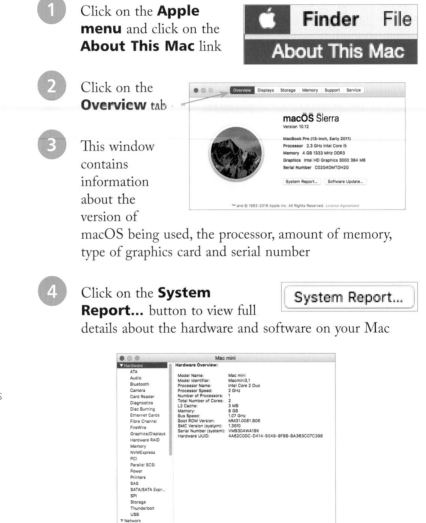

2 Click on the **Overview** tab

3 This window contains information about the version of macOS being used, the processor, amount of memory, type of graphics card and serial number

4 Click on the **System Report...** button to view full details about the hardware and software on your Mac

System Report...

Hot tip

The System Report section is also where you can check whether your Mac is compatible with the Handoff functionality, which does not work with most pre-2012 Macs. Click on the **Bluetooth** section in the **System Report** to see if Handoff is supported.

5 Click on the **Software Update...** button to see available software updates for your Mac

For more information about Software Updates, see page 181.

Display information

This gives information about your Mac's display:

1 Click on the **Displays** tab

Displays

2 This window contains information about your Mac's display, including the type, size, resolution and graphics card

Built-in Display
13.3-inch (1280 x 800)
Intel HD Graphics 3000 384 MB

Displays Preferences...

For more information about changing the resolution, see page 22.

13

3 Click on the **Displays Preferences...**

Displays Preferences...

button to view options for changing the display's resolution, brightness and color

Built-in Display | Q Search

Display | Color

Resolution: ○ Best for display
○ Scaled

Brightness: ————————●——

☑ Automatically adjust brightness

☑ Show mirroring options in the menu bar when available

14

Click on the **Manage...** button in the Storage window to view how much space specific apps are taking up, and also options for optimizing storage on your Mac. With macOS Sierra, this is known as **Optimized Storage**. Optimized Storage includes a **Store in iCloud** option, which can be used to enable your Mac to identify files that have not been opened or used in a long time, and then automatically store them in iCloud (if you have enough storage space there). Their location remains the same on your Mac, but they are physically kept in iCloud, thus freeing up more space on your Mac. Optimized Storage also has options for removing iTunes movies and TV shows that have been watched, emptying the Trash automatically and reducing overall clutter on your Mac.

...cont'd

Storage information

This contains information about your Mac's physical and removable storage:

 Click on the **Storage** tab   Storage

2 This window contains information about the used and available storage on your hard disk, and also options for writing various types of CDs and DVDs (if applicable)

Overview Displays **Storage** Memory Support Service

Macintosh HD
150.14 GB available of 317.09 GB   Manage...

Documents

320 GB
SATA Disk

Disc formats that can be written:
CD-R, CD-RW, DVD-R, DVD+R, DVD-RW, DVD+RW, DVD-R DL, DVD+R DL

SuperDrive

Memory information

This contains information about your Mac's memory, which is used to run macOS and also the applications on your computer:

1 Click on the **Memory** tab   Memory

2 This window contains information about the memory chips that are in your Mac

Overview Displays Storage **Memory** Support Service

8 GB
Installed

Your Mac contains 2 memory slots, each of which accepts a 1067 MHz DDR3 memory module.

All memory slots are currently in use.

4 GB   4 GB

Ⓘ Memory Upgrade Instructions

3 Click on **Memory Upgrade Instructions** if you want to upgrade your memory

Beware

Always wear an anti-static wristband if you are opening your Mac to insert new memory chips, or whenever you are working on the components of your Mac. This will prevent a build-up of static electricity which could short-circuit the parts and cause permanent damage.

4 A page on the Apple website opens, and gives instructions for upgrading memory chips for different makes and models of Macs

Support

The **Support** tab provides links to a range of help options for your Mac and macOS.

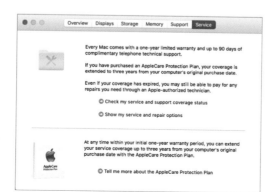

Service

The **Service** tab provides links to service and repair options and also the AppleCare Protection Plan, for extending the initial one-year warranty of your Mac.

About System Preferences

macOS Sierra has a wide range of options for customizing and configuring the way that your Mac operates. These are located within the System Preferences section. To access this:

For more detailed information about the Dock, see Chapter Two.

For a detailed look at System Preferences, see pages 38-39.

The **General** option in System Preferences can be used to change the overall appearance of macOS Sierra, including colors for buttons, menus, scroll bars and windows. Another option in System Preferences is for **Desktop & Screen Saver**. This has tabs for these items, from which you can select a background wallpaper for your Mac and also a screen saver for when it is inactive.

1 Click on this button on the Dock (the bar of icons that appears along the bottom of the screen), or access it from the Applications folder

2 All of the options are shown in the **System Preferences** window

3 Click once on an item to open it in the main System Preferences window. Each item will have a number of options for customization

4 Click on the **Show All** button to return to the main System Preferences window

Search Options

Finding items on a Mac or on the web is an important part of everyday computing, and with macOS Sierra there are a number of options for doing this:

Siri

Siri is Apple's digital voice assistant that can search for items using speech. It has been available on Apple's mobile devices using iOS for a number of years, and with macOS Sierra it is now available on Mac desktops and laptops. See pages 18-21 for more details about setting up and using Siri.

Spotlight search

Spotlight is the dedicated search app for macOS. It can be used over all the files on your Mac and the internet. To use Spotlight:

1. Click on this icon at the right of the Apple Menu bar

2. Click in the Spotlight Search box

3. Enter a keyword, or phrase, for which you want to search

4. The top hits from within your apps are shown in the left-hand panel. Click on one to view its details

5. Scroll down the left-hand panel to view different search result options, such as entries from Wikipedia, the web or a dictionary definition of a word

Finder search

This is the search box in the top right-hand corner of the Finder and can be used to search for items within it. See page 66 for details about using Finder search.

Beware

Spotlight starts searching for items as soon as you start typing a word. So don't worry if some of the first results look inappropriate, as these will disappear once you have finished typing the full word.

Don't forget

Spotlight search can show results from your Mac, the internet, iTunes, the App Store and also items such as movies nearby and local restaurants. These are displayed on a map within the Spotlight search results.

Using Siri

Now available with macOS Sierra, Siri is the digital voice assistant that can be used to vocally search for a wide range of items from your Mac and the web. Also, the results can be managed in innovative ways so that keeping up-to-date is easier than ever.

Setting up Siri

To set up and start using Siri:

1 Open **System Preferences** and click on the **Siri** button

2 Check **On** the **Enable Siri** box

Hot tip

Check **On** the **Show Siri in menu bar** box to show the Siri icon in the top right-hand corner of the main Apple Menu bar.

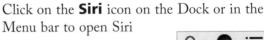

3 Make selections here for how Siri operates, including language and the voice used by Siri

4 Click on the **Siri** icon on the Dock or in the Menu bar to open Siri

Hot tip

An internal or external microphone is required in order to ask Siri questions.

5 The Siri window opens, ready for use

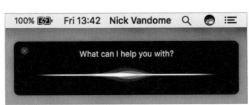

Searching with Siri

Siri can respond to most requests, including playing a music track, checking the weather, opening photos and adding calendar events. If you open Siri but do not ask a question, it will prompt you with a list of possible queries. Click on the microphone icon at the bottom of the panel to ask a question. It is also possible to ask questions of Siri while you are working on another document.

Siri can search for a vast range of items, from your Mac or the web. Some useful Siri functions include:

Searching for documents
This can be refined by specifying documents covering a specific date or subject:

1. Ask Siri to find and display documents with a criteria, e.g. created by a specific person

2. Ask Siri to refine the criteria, e.g. only include documents from a specific date range. Click on an item to open it in its related app

It is possible to ask Siri to search for specific types of documents, e.g. those created in Pages, or PDF files.

Don't forget

Click on the cross in the top left-hand corner of the Siri window to close it. Otherwise, it can be left open for more queries and searches.

...cont'd

Drag and drop results

Once search results have been displayed by Siri they can be managed in a variety of ways. One of these is to copy an item in the search results into another app, by dragging and dropping:

1 Ask Siri to display a certain type of item, such as a map location or an image

2 Drag the resulting item into another app, such as a word processing app or the Notes app

Multitasking

The Siri search window can be left open on the Desktop so that you can ask Siri a question while you are working on something else, e.g. while you are working on a document, ask Siri to display a relevant web page.

Pinning results

Some search results are dynamic, i.e. they change on a regular basis. This includes items such as sports results and weather forecasts. With Siri, these can be pinned to the Notification Center and they will then be updated when they change. To pin Siri search results:

 Search for a certain item, such as the results of your favorite sports team

When Siri returns the result, click on this button to pin the search to the Notification Center

The item will be pinned to the Notification Center, which will always display the most recent information, and it will be updated when new details are available

Hot tip

For more information about using the Notification Center, see pages 120-121.

Changing the Resolution

For most computer users, the size at which items are displayed on the screen is an important issue: if items are too small, this can make them hard to read and lead to eye strain; too large, and you have to spend a lot of time scrolling around to see everything.

The size of items on the screen is controlled by the screen's resolution, i.e. the number of colored dots displayed in an area of the screen. The higher the resolution, the smaller the items on the screen; the lower the resolution, the larger the items. To change the screen resolution:

Don't forget

A higher resolution makes items appear sharper on the screen, even though they appear physically smaller.

22

1 Click on this button in the **System Preferences** folder

Displays

2 Click on the **Display** tab

Display

3 Click on the **Default for display** button to let your Mac select the most appropriate resolution

4 Drag this slider to change the screen brightness. Check On the box underneath it to have this done automatically

5 Click on the **Scaled** option and select a resolution setting to change the overall screen resolution

| Display | Color |

Resolution: ⬤ Default for display
⬤ Scaled

1280 × 800
1152 × 720
1024 × 640

6 Click on the **Color** tab to select options for using different color profiles and also calibrating your monitor

Color

Accessibility

In all areas of computing it is important to give as many people access to the system as possible. This includes users with visual impairments and also people who have problems using the mouse and keyboard. In macOS this is achieved through the functions of the Accessibility section of System Preferences. To use these:

 Click on this button in the **System Preferences** folder

 Click on the **Display** option to change the settings for display colors, contrast, and to increase the cursor size

 Click on the **Zoom** option to change the settings for zooming in on the screen

Experiment with the VoiceOver function, if only to see how it operates. This will give you a better idea of how visually impaired users access information on a computer.

 Click on the **VoiceOver** option to enable VoiceOver, which provides a spoken description of what is on the screen

In macOS Sierra, the VoiceOver function has support for iBooks.

...cont'd

5 Click on the **Audio** option to select an on-screen flash for alerts, and settings for how sound is played

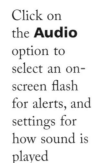

The Audio, Keyboard, and Mouse & Trackpad Accessibility options have links to additional options within their own System Preferences.

6 Click on the **Keyboard** option to access settings for customizing the keyboard

Another option in the Accessibility window is for **Switch Control**, which enables a Mac to be controlled by a variety of devices including the mouse, keypad and gamepad devices.

7 Click on the **Mouse & Trackpad** option to access settings for customizing these devices

8 Click on the **Dictation** option to select preferences for using spoken commands

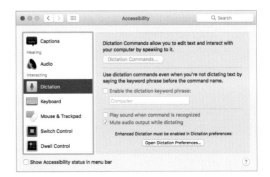

The Spoken Word

macOS Sierra not only has numerous apps for adding text to documents, emails and messages; it also has a Dictation function so that you can speak what you want to appear on screen. To set up and use the Dictation feature:

1 Click on the **Dictation** tab in **System Preferences** > **Keyboard**

2 Click the **On** button to enable Dictation

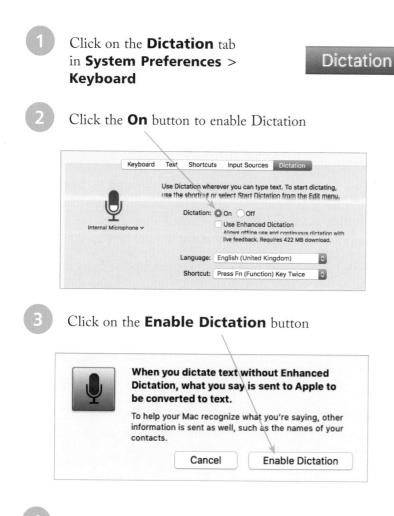

3 Click on the **Enable Dictation** button

When you dictate text without Enhanced Dictation, what you say is sent to Apple to be converted to text.

To help your Mac recognize what you're saying, other information is sent as well, such as the names of your contacts.

Cancel   Enable Dictation

4 Once Dictation has been turned On, it can be accessed in relevant apps by selecting **Edit** > **Start Dictation** from the Menu bar

Start Dictation

5 Start talking when the microphone icon appears. Click **Done** when you have finished recording your text

Hot tip

Punctuation can be added with the Dictation function, by speaking commands such as 'comma' or 'question mark'. These will then be converted into the appropriate symbols.

Don't forget

Dictation settings can also be found in **System Preferences** > **Accessibility** – see Step 8 on the previous page.

Shutting Down

The Apple menu (which can be accessed by clicking on the Apple icon at the top left corner of the Desktop, or any subsequent macOS window) is standardized in macOS. This means that it has the same options regardless of the app in which you are working. This has a number of advantages, not least is the fact that it makes it easier to shut down your Mac. When shutting down, there are three options that can be selected:

When shutting down, make sure you have saved all of your open documents, although macOS will prompt you to do this if you have forgotten.

- **Sleep**. This puts the Mac into hibernation mode, i.e. the screen goes blank and the hard drive becomes inactive. This state is maintained until the mouse is moved or a key is pressed on the keyboard. This then wakes up the Mac and it is ready to continue work. It is a good idea to add a login password for accessing the Mac when it wakes up, otherwise other people could wake it up and gain access to it. To add a login password, go to **System Preferences** > **Security & Privacy** and click on the **General** tab. Check On the **Require password** checkbox and select from one of the timescale options (**immediately** is best).

If a password is added, the Lock screen will appear whenever the Mac is woken from sleep and the password will be required to unlock it.

- **Restart**. This closes down the Mac and then restarts it again. This can be useful if you have added new software and your computer requires a restart to make it active.

- **Shut Down**. This closes down the Mac completely once you have finished working.

Users of the Apple Watch can unlock their Mac running macOS Sierra, without a password.

macOS Sierra has a **Resume** function where the Mac opens up in the same state as when it was shut down. See page 54 for details.

Click here to access the **Apple menu**

Click here to access one of the shut down options

Finder	File	Edit	View	

About This Mac

System Preferences...
Location   ▶
App Store...

Recent Items   ▶

Force Quit Finder   ⌥⇧⌘⌫

Sleep
Restart...
Shut Down...

Log Out Nick Vandome...   ⇧⌘Q

2 Getting Up and Running

This chapter looks at some of the essential features of macOS Sierra. These include the Dock for organizing and accessing all of the elements of your Mac computer, the System Preferences for the way your Mac looks and operates, and items for arranging folders and files. It also introduces the online sharing service, iCloud, for sharing your digital content, including the Family Sharing feature for sharing your photos, music, apps and books with family members.

28   Introducing the Dock

29   Apps on the Dock

30   Setting Dock Preferences

32   Stacks on the Dock

34   Dock Menus

35   Working with Dock Items

37   Trash

38   System Preferences

40   About iCloud

41   Setting up iCloud

42   About the iCloud Drive

44   Continuity

45   Handoff

46   About Family Sharing

48   Using Family Sharing

52   Desktop Items

53   Ejecting Items

54   Resuming

Introducing the Dock

The Dock is one of the main organizational elements of macOS. Its main function is to help organize and access apps, folders and files. In addition, with its background and icons, it also makes an aesthetically pleasing addition to the Desktop. The main things to remember about the Dock are:

Don't forget

The Dock is always displayed as a line of icons, but this can be orientated either vertically or horizontally.

● It is divided into two: apps go on the left of the dividing line; all other items go on the right.

● It can be customized in several different ways.

By default, the Dock appears at the bottom of the screen:

Hot tip

Items on the Dock can be opened by clicking on them once, rather than having to double-click them. Once they have been accessed, the icon bobs up and down until the item is available.

Apps go here   Dividing line   Open items

By default, the two icons to the right of the dividing line are:

Hot tip

The Downloads icon can be displayed as a Folder or a Stack (see pages 32-33). To set this, Ctrl + click on the Download icon and select either **Folder** or **Stack** under the **Display as** option.

Downloads. This is for items that you have downloaded from the web. The items can be accessed from here and opened or run.

Trash. This is where items can be dragged to if you want to remove them. It can also be used to eject removable devices, such as flashdrives, by dragging the device's icon over the Trash. It cannot be removed from the Dock.

Apps on the Dock

Opening apps

When you open apps they appear on the Dock and can be worked with within the Dock environment.

1 Click once on an app to open it (either on the Dock, in the Finder Applications folder or the Launchpad). Once an app has been opened, it is displayed on the Dock with a black dot underneath it

2 When windows are opened within the app, they are displayed to the right of the dividing line

3 Click on an icon to the right of the dividing line to maximize it: it disappears from the Dock and displays at full size

4 If a window is minimized by clicking on this button, it goes back to the right-hand side of the dividing line on the Dock

5 Press and hold underneath an open app to view the available windows for the app (this will differ for individual apps as some operate by using a single window)

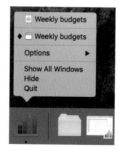

6 To close an open app, press and hold on the black dot underneath its icon on the Dock and click on the **Quit** button (or select its name on the Menu bar and select **Quit**)

Apps can be opened from the Dock, the Finder or the Launchpad. The Finder is covered in detail in Chapter Three, and see pages 100-101 for more on the Launchpad.

Some apps such as Notes, Reminders and Calendar, will close when the active window is closed. Others such as Pages, Keynote and Numbers, will remain open even if all of the windows are closed: the recently-accessed documents will be displayed as in the context menu in Step 5.

Setting Dock Preferences

As with most elements of macOS, the Dock can be modified in numerous ways. This can affect both the appearance of the Dock and the way it operates. To set Dock preferences:

 Select **System Preferences** > **Dock**

Dock

 The Dock Preferences allow you to change its size, orientation, the way icons appear with magnification, and effects for when items are minimized

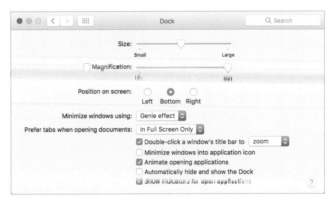

 Drag the Dock **Size** slider to increase or decrease the size of the Dock

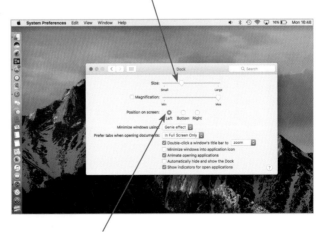

The **Position on screen** options enable you to place the Dock on the left, right or bottom of the screen

Beware

The Dock cannot be moved by dragging it physically; this can only be done in the Dock Preferences window.

Beware

You cannot make the Dock size so large that some of the icons would not be visible on the Desktop. By default, the Dock is resized so that everything is always visible.

4 Click on the **Magnification** box and drag the slider to determine the size to which icons are enlarged when the cursor is moved over them

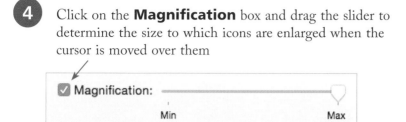

Move the cursor over an icon on the Dock to see the magnification effect.

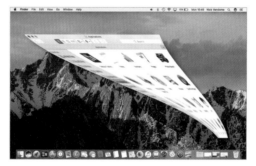

5 The **Genie effect** under the **Minimize windows using** option shrinks the item to be minimized, like a genie going back into its lamp

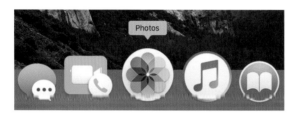

Hot tip

Open windows can also be minimized by double-clicking on the Title bar (the area at the top of the window, next to the three window buttons).

31

Manual resizing

In addition to changing the size of the Dock by using the Dock Preference dialog box, it can also be resized manually:

1 Drag vertically on the Dock dividing line to increase or decrease its size

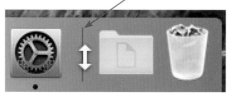

Stacks on the Dock

Stacking items

To save space, it is possible to add folders to the Dock, where their contents can easily be accessed. This is known as Stacks. By default, Stacks for downloaded files are created on the Dock. To use Stacks:

When the cursor is moved over an item in the Dock, the name of that item is displayed above it.

 To create a new Stack, drag a folder onto the Dock. Stacked items are placed on the right of the Dock dividing line

2 Click on a Stack to view its contents

3 Stacks can be viewed as:

- A grid

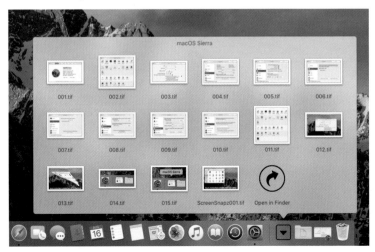

...cont'd

- A fan, depending on the number of items it contains

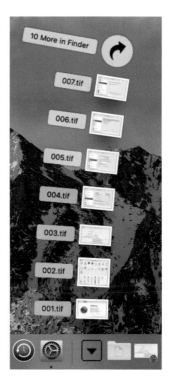

Move the cursor over a Stack, then press Ctrl + click to access options for how that Stack is displayed.

- A list. Click on a folder to view its contents within a Stack, then click on files to open them in their relevant app

Any new items that are added to the folder will also be visible through the Stack

Dock Menus

One of the features of the Dock is that it can display contextual menus for selected items. This means that it shows menus with options that are applicable to the item that is being accessed. This can only be done when an item has been opened.

1 Click and hold on the black dot underneath an item's icon to display the item's individual context menu

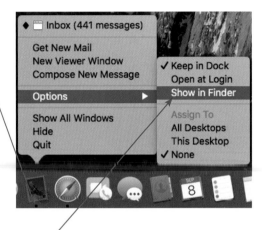

Hot tip

Click on **Quit** on the icon's contextual menu to close an open app or file, depending on which side of the dividing bar the item is located.

2 Click on **Show in Finder** to see where the item is located on your computer

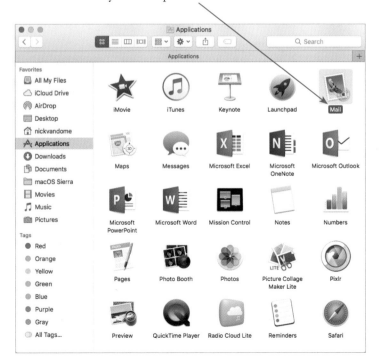

Working with Dock Items

Adding items

Numerous items can be added to the Dock; the only restriction is the size of monitor on which to display all of the Dock items. (The size of the Dock can be reduced to accommodate more icons, but you have to be careful that all of the icons are still legible.) To add items to the Dock:

Don't forget

If you are upgrading to macOS Sierra (rather than buying a new Mac), the Dock setup will be the same as the one used with the previous version of the operating system.

1 Locate the required item in the Finder and drag it onto the Dock. All of the other icons move along to make space for the new one

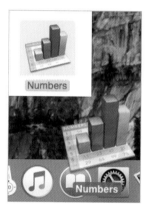

Don't forget

Icons on the Dock are shortcuts to the related item, rather than the item itself, which remains in its original location.

Keep in Dock

Every time you open a new app, its icon will appear in the Dock for the duration that the app is open, even if it has not previously been put in the Dock. If you then decide that you would like to keep it in the Dock, you can enable this as follows:

Beware

You can add numerous items to the Dock, but it will automatically shrink to display all of its items if it becomes too big for the available space.

1 Click and hold on the black dot underneath an open app's icon

2 Select **Options > Keep in Dock** to ensure the app remains in the Dock when it is closed

...cont'd

Removing items

Any item, except the Finder, can be removed from the Dock. However, this does not remove it from your computer, it just removes the shortcut for accessing it. You will still be able to locate it in its folder in the Finder, and if required, drag it back onto the Dock. To remove items from the Dock:

Hot tip

When an icon is dragged from the Dock, it has to be moved a reasonable distance before the Remove alert appears.

 Drag the item away from the Dock until it displays the **Remove** tag. The item disappears once the cursor is released. All of the other icons then move up to fill in the space

Removing open apps

You can remove an app from the Dock, even if it is open and running. To do this:

 Drag an app off the Dock while it is running. Initially the icon will remain on the Dock because the app is still open

Don't forget

If **Keep in Dock** has been selected for an item (see page 35) the app will remain in the Dock even when it has been closed.

 When the app is closed (click and hold on the dot underneath the item and select **Quit**) its icon will be removed from the Dock

Trash

The Trash folder is a location for placing items that you do not need anymore. However, when items are placed in the Trash, they are not removed from your computer. This requires another command, as the Trash is really a holding area before you decide you want to remove items permanently. The Trash can also be used for ejecting removable disks attached to your Mac.

Sending items to the Trash
Items can be sent to the Trash by dragging them from the location in which they are stored.

 Drag an item over the **Trash** icon to place it in the Trash folder

Items can also be sent to the Trash by selecting them in the Finder and then selecting **File** > **Move to Trash** from the Menu bar.

Click once on the **Trash** icon on the Dock to view its contents

All of the items within the Trash can be removed in a single command: Select **Finder** > **Empty Trash** from the Menu bar to remove all of the items in the Trash folder.

System Preferences

In macOS there are preferences that can be set for just about every aspect of your computer. This gives you greater control over how the interface looks and how the operating system functions. To access System Preferences:

 Click on this icon on the Dock or from the Applications folder in the Finder

Personal preferences

General. Options for the overall look of buttons, menus, windows and scroll bars.

Desktop & Screen Saver. This can be used to change the Desktop background and the screen saver.

Dock. Options for the way the Dock looks and functions.

Mission Control. This gives you a variety of options for managing all of your open windows and apps.

Language & Region. Options for the language used on your Mac.

Security & Privacy. This enables you to secure your Home folder with a master password, for added security.

Spotlight. This can be used to specify settings for the macOS search facility, Spotlight.

Notifications. This can be used to set up how you are notified about items such as email, messages and software updates.

Hardware preferences

CDs & DVDs. Options for what action is taken when you insert CDs and DVDs (if there is a SuperDrive).

Displays. Options for the screen display, such as resolution.

Energy Saver. Options for when the computer is inactive.

Keyboard. Options for how the keyboard functions, your keyboard shortcuts and dictation settings.

Mouse. Options for how the mouse functions.

Trackpad. Options for when you are using a trackpad.

Printers & Scanners. Options for selecting printers and scanners.

The SuperDrive is an internal drive on some Macs, which can be used to play and burn CDs and DVDs. However, it is not available on many new Macs so an external one can be used instead, with a USB connection.

macOS Sierra supports multiple displays, which means you can connect your Mac to two or more displays and view different content on each one. The Dock appears on the active screen and each screen also has its own Menu bar. Different full screen apps can also be viewed on each screen.

Sound. Options for adding sound effects and playing and recording sound.

Startup Disk. This can be used to specify the disk from which your computer starts up. This is usually the macOS volume.

Internet & Wireless preferences

iCloud. Options for the online iCloud service.

Internet Accounts. This can be used to link to other online accounts that you have (see tip).

App Store. This can be used to specify how software updates are handled. It connects to the App Store to access the available updates.

Network. This can be used to specify network settings for connecting to the internet or other computers.

Bluetooth. Options for attaching Bluetooth wireless devices.

Extensions. This can be used to customize your Mac with extensions and plug-ins from Apple and third-party developers.

Sharing. This can be used to specify how files are shared over a network. This is also covered on page 169.

System preferences

Users & Groups. This can be used to create accounts for different users on your Mac.

Parental Controls. This can be used to limit access to the computer and various online functions.

Siri. This can be used to turn on or off the digital voice assistant, Siri, and also set voice style and language.

Date & Time. Options for changing the computer's date and time to time zones around the world.

Time Machine. This can be used to configure and set up the macOS backup facility.

Accessibility. This can be used to set options for users who have difficulty with viewing text on screen, hearing commands, using the keyboard or using the mouse.

The **Internet Accounts** section can be used to set up email accounts and also link to your social networking accounts such as Facebook, Twitter and LinkedIn.

Two useful extensions that can be added are DivX and Flash Player, both of which can be used to play certain types of video content, particularly on the web.

About iCloud

Cloud computing is an attractive proposition and one that has gained great popularity in recent years. As a concept, it consists of storing your content on an external computer server. This not only gives you added security in terms of backing up your information, it also means that the content can then be shared over a variety of devices.

iCloud is Apple's consumer Cloud computing product that consists of online services such as email, a calendar, notes, contacts and saving photos and documents. iCloud provides users with a way to save and backup their files and content to the online service and then use them across their Apple devices such as other Mac computers, iPhones, iPads and iPod Touches.

About iCloud
iCloud can be set up from this icon within System Preferences:

There is also a version of iCloud for Windows, which can be accessed for download from the Apple website at **www.apple.com/icloud/setup/pc.html**

You can use iCloud to save and share the following between your different devices, with an Apple ID account (see next page):

- Photos

- Mail and Safari

- Documents

- Backups

- Notes

- Reminders

- Contacts and Calendar

When you save an item to iCloud it automatically pushes it to all of your other compatible devices; you do not have to manually sync anything, iCloud does it all for you.

Setting up iCloud

To use iCloud with macOS Sierra you need to first have an Apple ID. This is a service you can register for to be able to access a range of Apple facilities, including iCloud. You can register with an email address and a password. When you first start using iCloud you will be prompted for your Apple ID details. If you do not have an Apple ID you can create one at this point.

 Sign in with your Apple ID, or

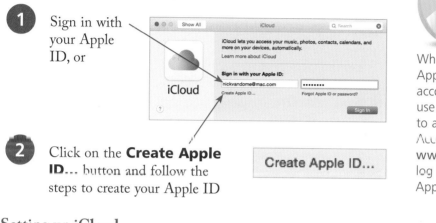

 Click on the **Create Apple ID...** button and follow the steps to create your Apple ID

Create Apple ID...

When you have an Apple ID and an iCloud account, you can also use the iCloud website to access your content. Access the website at **www.icloud.com** and log in with your Apple ID details.

Setting up iCloud
To use iCloud:

 Open System Preferences and click on the **iCloud** button

iCloud

 Check on the items you want included within iCloud. All of these items will be backed up and shared across all of your Apple devices

The online iCloud service includes your online email service, Contacts, Calendar, Reminders, Notes and versions of Pages, Keynote and Numbers. You can log in to your iCloud account from any internet-enabled device.

About the iCloud Drive

One of the options in the iCloud section is for the iCloud Drive. This can be used to store documents and other content so that you can use them on any other Apple devices that you have, such as an iPhone or an iPad. With the iCloud Drive you can start work on a document on one device, and continue on another device from where you left off. To set up the iCloud Drive:

 Click on the **iCloud** button in System Preferences

Check **On** the **iCloud Drive** option and click on the **Options...** button

Select the items to use with the iCloud Drive. In macOS Sierra, this includes the **Desktop & Documents Folders** option, which ensures that any items saved into these locations will be stored in the iCloud Drive

Click on the **Done** button

Beware

If the **Desktop & Documents Folders** option is selected for the iCloud Drive this can take up a lot of iCloud storage, as all items in these locations will be saved to the iCloud Drive, which counts towards your iCloud storage limit.

Using the iCloud Drive
To work with files in the iCloud Drive:

 In the Finder sidebar click on the **iCloud Drive** button

2 Certain iCloud Drive folders are already created, based on the apps that you have selected on the previous page. These are the default folders into which content from their respective apps will be placed (although others can also be selected, if required). Double-click on a folder to view its contents

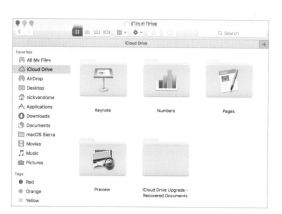

3 To save files into an iCloud Drive folder, select **File > Save As** from the Menu bar, click on the **iCloud Drive** button in the Finder sidebar and navigate to the required folder for the file

Don't forget

Pages is the Apple app for word processing, Numbers for spreadsheets and Keynote for presentations. These can all be downloaded from the App Store, if they do not come preinstalled on your Mac.

Hot tip

Another useful iCloud function is the iCloud Keychain (**System Preferences** > **iCloud** and check on the **Keychain** option). If this is enabled, it can keep all of your passwords and credit card information up-to-date across multiple devices and remember them when you use them on websites. The information is encrypted and controlled through your Apple ID.

Continuity

One of the themes of macOS Sierra and iOS for mobile devices (iOS 8 and later) is to make all of your content available on all of your Apple devices. This is known as Continuity: when you create something on one device you can then pick it up and finish it on another. This is done through iCloud. To do this:

 Ensure the app has iCloud activated, as on page 41

 Create the content in the app on your Mac

3 Open the same app on another Apple device, e.g. an iPad. The item created on your Mac should be available to view and edit. Any changes will then show up on the file on your Mac too

Hot tip

It is also possible to continue an email with the Continuity feature. First, create it on your Mac and then close it. You will be prompted to save the email as a draft and, if you do this, you will be able to open it from the **Drafts** mailbox on another Apple device.

Handoff

Handoff is one of the key features of Continuity and it displays icons of items that you have opened on other devices, such as Safari web pages. Handoff does not work with all devices; it only works if both devices have OS X Yosemite or later, and iOS 8 or later, for mobile devices.

To use Handoff you will need to do the following:

- Your Mac must be running OS X Yosemite (or later) and your mobile device (iPhone 5 and later, iPad Pro, iPad 4 and later, all models of iPad mini and the 5th generation iPod Touch) must have iOS 8 (or later).

- Your Mac has to support Bluetooth 4.0, which means that most pre-2012 Macs are not compatible with Handoff.

To check if your Mac supports Handoff:

 Select **Apple Menu** > **About This Mac** > **System Report**. Click on **Bluetooth** to see if Handoff is supported

Bluetooth Low Energy Supported:	Yes
Handoff Supported:	Yes
Instant Hotspot Supported:	Yes

2 Turn on Bluetooth on your Mac (via System Preferences) and on your mobile device (via Settings)

3 Turn on Handoff on your Mac (**System Preferences > General** and check on **Allow Handoff Between this Mac and your iCloud Devices**) and on your mobile device (**Settings > General > Handoff**)

4 When Handoff is activated, compatible apps will be displayed at the left-hand side of the Dock when they have been opened on another device

The apps that work with Handoff are Mail, Safari, Maps, Messages, Reminders, Calendar, Contacts, Notes, Pages, Numbers and Keynote.

If Handoff is not working, try turning both devices off and on and do the same with Bluetooth. Also, try logging out, and then back in, to your iCloud account on both devices.

About Family Sharing

As everyone gets more and more digital devices it is becoming increasingly important to be able to share content with other people, particularly family members. In macOS Sierra, and iCloud, the Family Sharing function enables you to share items that you have downloaded from the App Store, such as music and movies, with up to six other family members, as long as they have an Apple ID. Once this has been set up it is also possible to share items such as family calendars, photos and even see where family members' devices are located. To set up Family Sharing:

To use Family Sharing, other family members must have an Apple device using either iOS 8 (or later) for a mobile device (iPad, iPhone or iPod Touch) or OS X Yosemite (or later) for a desktop or laptop Mac computer.

1 Click on the **iCloud** button in System Preferences

2 Click on the **Set Up Family** (or the **Manage Family** button if Family Sharing has already been set up)

3 One person will be the organizer of Family Sharing, i.e. in charge of it, and if you set it up then it will be you. Click on the **+** button to add other family members

4 Enter the name or email address of a family member

> **Add a family member**
>
> ● Enter a family member's name or email address.
>
> Lucy Vandome <lavme@hotmail.co.uk>
>
> ○ Create an Apple ID for a child who doesn't have an account.
>
> Cancel   Continue

and click on the **Continue** button

5 Verify your debit or credit card information for your iCloud account,

> **Verify the security code on your card.**
>
> This payment method will be used to pay for purchases initiated by your family members.
>
> Security code for Visa (•••• ▮▮▮▮): ▮▮▮
>
> Go Back   Continue

as this will be used by the family member for making purchases. Click on the **Continue** button

6 Enter your Apple ID password and click on the **Continue** button

> **Enter your password to make changes to your account.**
>
> null
>
> Password: ••••••••   Forgot?
>
> Cancel   Continue

7 An invitation is sent to the selected person. They have to accept this before

> Nick Vando... (Me)
> Organizer
> Eilidh Vandome
> Age 17
> Lucy Vandome
> Invitation sent
>
> LV
>
> **Lucy Vandome**
> lavme@hotmail.co.uk
>
> Lucy has not yet accepted your invitation.
>
> Resend Invitation
>
> + −   Done

they can participate in Family Sharing

If children are part of the Family Sharing group you can specify that they need your permission before downloading any items from the iTunes Store, the App Store or the iBooks Store. To do this, click on **iCloud** in **System Preferences** and click on the **Manage Family** button. Select a family member and check **On** the **Ask to Buy** button. You will then receive a notification whenever they want to buy something, and you can either allow or deny their request.

Using Family Sharing

Once Family Sharing has been set up it can be used by members of the group to share music, apps, movies and books. There is also a shared Family calendar that can be used, and it is also possible to view the location of the devices of the family members.

Sharing music

To share music, and other content from the iTunes Store, such as movies and TV shows:

1 Click on the **iTunes** app on the Dock

2 Click on the **Purchased** link

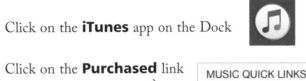

Hot tip

You have to be connected to the internet and online to access the iTunes Store and view purchases from other family members. When you do this, you can play their songs without having to download them. However, if you want to be able to use them when you are offline then you will have to download them first, as in Step 5.

3 By default, your own purchases are displayed. Click on the drop-down option next to the **Purchased** button to view other members of Family Sharing

4 Click on another family member to view their purchases (they will be able to do this for your purchases too)

5 Click on the iCloud button to download the other family member's music tracks or albums to your device

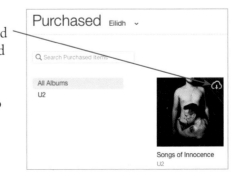

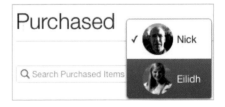

Sharing apps

Apps can also be shared from the App Store. To do this:

1 Click on the **App Store** app on the Dock

2 Click on the **Purchased** button

3 By default, your own purchases are displayed. Click on the **My Purchases** drop-down to view other members of Family Sharing

4 Click on another family member to view and then download their purchased apps (they will be able to do this for your apps too)

Sharing books

Books can also be shared in a similar way to items from the iTunes Store and the App Store. To do this:

1 Click on the **iBooks** app on the Dock

2 Click on the **iBooks Store** button

 iBooks Store

3 Click on the **Purchased** link, under the **Quick Links** heading

QUICK LINKS
Account
Purchased

4 By default, your own purchases are displayed. Click on the **Purchased** account drop-down option to view other members of Family Sharing and any books they have downloaded

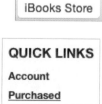

Don't forget

More than one family member can use content in the Family Sharing group at the same time.

...cont'd

Sharing calendars

Family Sharing also generates a Family calendar that can be used by all Family Sharing members:

Other members of the Family Sharing group can add items to the Family calendar and, when they do, you will be sent a notification that appears on your Mac.

To change the color of a calendar, click on the **Calendars** button at the top left of the window. Ctrl + click on a calendar name, and select a color from the bottom of the panel, or click on **Custom Color...** to choose from the full spectrum.

1 Open the **Calendar** app

2 Double-click on a date to create a **New Event**. The current calendar (shown in the top right-hand corner) will probably not be the Family one. Click on this button to change the calendar

3 Click on the **Family** calendar

- ✓ ☐ Home
- ☐ IES
- ■ Work
- ■ Birthdays
- ☐ Family
- ■ Emma
- ■ Squash/Tennis
- ■ Lucy
- ☐ Eilidh

4 Complete the details for the event. It will be added to your calendar, with the Family color tag. Other people in your Family Sharing circle will have this event added to their Family calendar, and they will also be sent a notification

Finding lost family devices

Family Sharing also makes it possible to see where everyone's devices are, which can be useful for locating people, but particularly so if a device belonging to a Family Sharing member is lost or stolen. To do this:

1 Ensure that the **Find My Mac** function is turned on in the **iCloud** System Preferences, and log in to your online iCloud account at **www.icloud.com**

2 Click on the **Find iPhone** button (this works for other Apple devices too)

3 Devices that are turned on, online and with iCloud activated are shown by green dots

Don't forget

The location of devices is shown on a map and you can zoom in on the map to see their location more accurately.

51

4 Click on a green dot to display information about the device. Click on the **i** symbol to access options for managing the device remotely

5 There are options to send an alert sound to the device, lock it remotely or erase its contents (if you are concerned about it having fallen into the wrong hands)

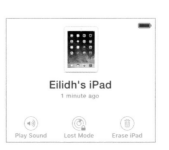

Desktop Items

If required, the Desktop can be used to store apps and files. However, the Finder (see Chapter Three) does such a good job of organizing all of the elements within your computer that the Desktop is rendered largely redundant, unless you feel happier storing items here. The Desktop can also display any removable disks that are connected to your computer:

Hot tip

Icons for removable disks, e.g. flashdrives, CDs or DVDs, will only become visible on the Desktop once a disk has been inserted.

If a removable disk is connected to your computer, double-click the desktop icon to view its contents

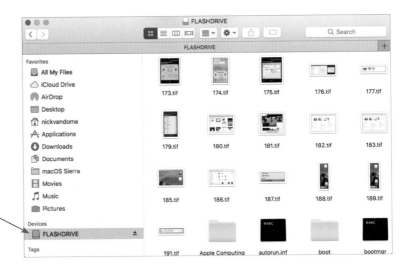

Don't forget

Any removable disks that are connected to your computer can also be viewed by clicking on them in the sidebar in the Finder.

Ejecting Items

If you have removable disks attached to your Mac it is essential to be able to eject them quickly and easily. In macOS there are two ways in which this can be done:

1 In the Finder, click on the icon to the right of the name of the removable disk, or

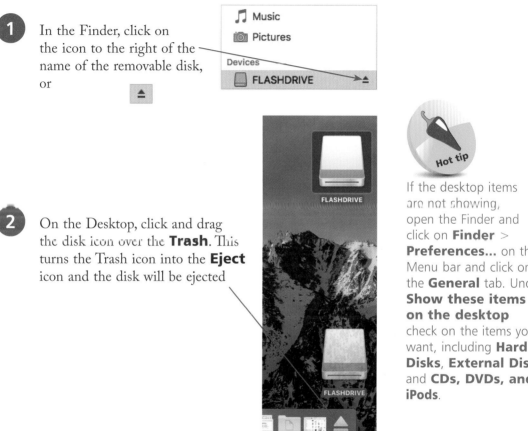

2 On the Desktop, click and drag the disk icon over the **Trash**. This turns the Trash icon into the **Eject** icon and the disk will be ejected

Hot tip

If the desktop items are not showing, open the Finder and click on **Finder > Preferences...** on the Menu bar and click on the **General** tab. Under **Show these items on the desktop** check on the items you want, including **Hard Disks**, **External Disks** and **CDs, DVDs, and iPods**.

3 Some disks, such as CDs and DVDs, are physically ejected when either of these two actions are performed. Other disks, such as flashdrives, have to be removed manually once they have been ejected by macOS. If the disk is not ejected first, the following warning message will appear:

Resuming

One of the chores about computing is that when you close down your computer, you have to first close down all of your open documents and apps and then open them all again when you turn your machine back on. However, macOS Sierra has a feature that allows you to continue working exactly where you left off, even if you turn off your computer. To do this:

 Before you close down, all of your open documents and apps are available (as shown)

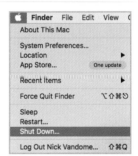

Beware

If you have open, unsaved documents you will be prompted to save them before your Mac is closed down.

 Select the **Shut Down...** or **Restart...** option from the **Apple menu**

 Make sure this box is checked on (this will ensure that all of your items will appear as before, after the Mac is closed down and then started up again)

4 Confirm the **Shut Down** or **Restart** command

3 Finder

The principal method for moving around macOS Sierra is the Finder. This enables you to access items and organize your apps, folders and files. This chapter looks at how to use the Finder and how to get the most out of this powerful tool which is at the heart of navigating around macOS. It covers accessing items, how to customize the interface, and numerous options for working with folders in macOS Sierra.

56 **Working with the Finder**

57 **Finder Folders**

59 **Finder Views**

62 **Covers**

63 **Quick Look**

64 **Finder Toolbar**

65 **Finder Sidebar**

66 **Finder Search**

67 **Copying and Moving Items**

68 **Working with Folders**

69 **Selecting Items**

70 **Finder Tabs**

72 **Tagging in the Finder**

74 **Spring-loaded Folders**

75 **Burnable Folders**

76 **Actions Button**

77 **Sharing from the Finder**

78 **Menus**

Working with the Finder

If you were only able to use one item on the Dock it would be the Finder. This is the gateway to all of the elements of your Mac. While it is possible to get to selected items through other routes, the Finder is the only location where you can gain access to everything on your system. If you ever feel that you are getting lost within macOS, click on the Finder and then you should begin to feel more at home. To access the Finder:

 Click once on this icon on the Dock

Overview

The Finder has its own toolbar, a sidebar from which items can be accessed, and a main window where the contents of selected items can be viewed:

Don't forget

A link to the iCloud Drive is also included in the Finder sidebar.

Don't forget

The Actions button has options for displaying information about a selected item and also options for how it is displayed within the Finder (see page 76 for details).

Forward and Back   Toolbar   View options   Actions button   Search

View all files

Folders are displayed here in the sidebar

Tags

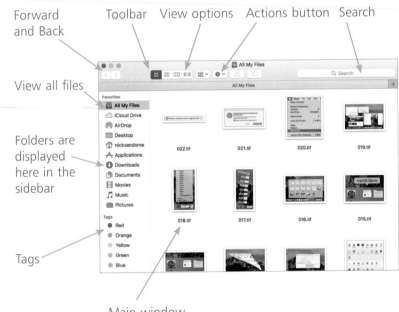

Main window

Finder Folders

All My Files

This contains all of the latest files in which you have been working. They are sorted into categories according to file type so that you can search through them quickly. This is an excellent way to locate items without having to look through a lot of folders. To access this:

1 Click on this link in the Finder sidebar to access the contents of your **All My Files** folder

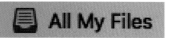

2 All of your files are displayed in individual categories. Click on the headings at the top of each category to sort items by those criteria

3 Double-click an item to open it from the Finder

The Finder is always open (as denoted by the black dot underneath its icon on the Dock) and it cannot readily be closed down or removed.

The Finder sidebar has the macOS Sierra transparency feature, so that you can see some of the open window, or Desktop, behind it.

To change the display of folders in the sidebar, click on the **Finder** menu on the top toolbar. Select **Preferences...** and click on the **Sidebar** tab. Under **Show these items in the sidebar:**, select the items you want included.

...cont'd

Home folder

This contains the contents of your own Home directory, containing your personal folders and files. macOS inserts some pre-named folders which it thinks will be useful, but it is possible to rearrange or delete these as you please. It is also possible to add as many more folders as you want.

Don't forget

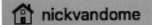

Applications

This folder contains all of the applications on your Mac. They can also be accessed from the Launchpad, as shown on page 100.

Documents

This is part of your Home folder but is put on the Finder sidebar for ease of access. New folders can be created for different types of documents.

1 Click on your Apple ID account name in the sidebar to access the contents of your **Home** folder

🏠 **nickvandome**

2 The Home folder contains the **Public** folder, which can be used to share files with other users if the computer is part of a network

Hot tip

When you are creating documents, macOS by default recognizes their type, and then when you save them, suggests the most applicable folder in which to save them.

3 To add a new folder, click the **Actions** button, then **New Folder**. The new folder will open in the main window, named "untitled folder". Overtype the name with one of your choice

4 To delete a folder from the Finder sidebar, Ctrl + click on it and select **Remove from Sidebar**

Finder Views

The way in which items are displayed within the Finder can be amended in a variety of ways, depending on how you want to view the contents of a folder. Different folders can have their own viewing options applied to them, and these will stay in place until a new option is specified.

Back button

When working within the Finder, each new window replaces the previous one, unless you open a new app. This prevents the screen becoming cluttered with dozens of open windows, as you look through various Finder windows for a particular item. To ensure that you never feel lost within the Finder structure, there is a Back button on the Finder toolbar that enables you to retrace the steps that you have taken.

Hot tip

Select an item within the Finder window and click on the space bar to view its details.

1. Navigate to a folder within the Finder (in this example, the **Madeira** folder contained within **Pictures**)

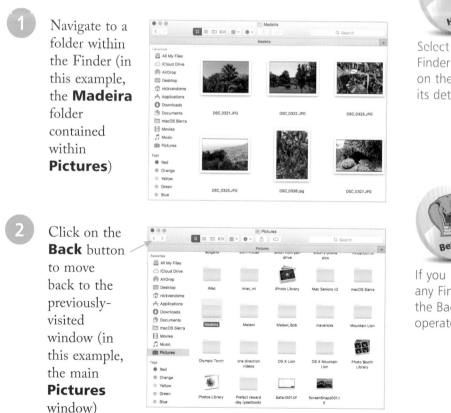

2. Click on the **Back** button to move back to the previously-visited window (in this example, the main **Pictures** window)

< >

Beware

If you have not opened any Finder windows, the Back button will not operate.

...cont'd

Icon view

One of the viewing options for displaying items within the Finder is as icons. This provides a pictorial representation of the items in the Finder. It is possible to customize the way that Icon view looks and functions.

The **Arrange By** options can be used to arrange icons into specific groups, e.g. by name or type, or to snap them to an invisible grid so that they have an ordered appearance.

① Click here on the Finder toolbar to access **Icon** view

② Select **View** from the Menu bar, check on **as Icons** and select **Show View Options** to access the options for customizing Icon view

A very large icon size can be useful for people with poor eyesight, but it does take up a lot more space in a window.

③ Drag this slider to set the icon size

④ Select an option for the way icons are arranged in Finder windows

⑤ Select an option for the background of the Finder window

List view

List view can be used to show the items within a Finder window as a list, with additional information shown next to them. This can be a more efficient method than Icon view if there are a lot of items within a folder, as List view enables you to see more items at one time and also view the additional information.

1 Click here on the Finder toolbar to access **List** view

2 The name of each folder or file is displayed here. If folders below the top-level folders have additional items within them, this is denoted by a small triangle next to them. Additional information in List view, such as file size and last modified date, is included in columns to the right

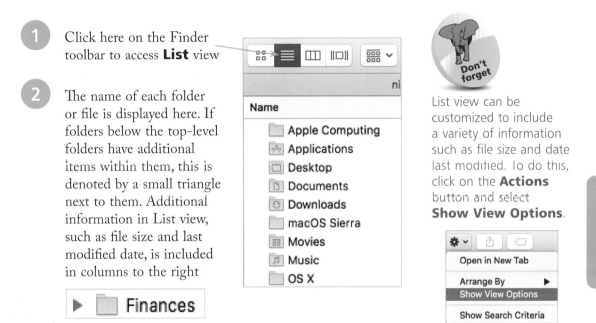

Don't forget

List view can be customized to include a variety of information such as file size and date last modified. To do this, click on the **Actions** button and select **Show View Options**.

61

Column view

Column view is a useful option if you want to trace the location of a particular item, i.e. see the full path of its location, starting from the hard drive:

1 Click here on the Finder toolbar to access **Column** view

2 Click on an item to see everything within that folder. If an arrow follows an item, it means that there are further items to view

Covers

Covers is a feature on the Mac which enables you to view items as large icons. This is particularly useful for image files, as it enables you to quickly see the details of the image to see if it is the one you want. To use Covers:

 Select a folder and at the top of the Finder window click on this button

 The items within the folder are displayed in their cover state

All files can be displayed in Covers view, including documents, music, apps and videos.

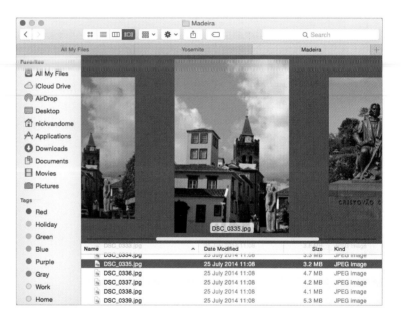

 Drag on the slider at the bottom of the window to move through the thumbnails. You can also move between items by swiping left or right on a trackpad or Magic Mouse

Quick Look

Through a Finder option called Quick Look, it is possible to view the content of a file without having to first open it. To do this:

 Select a file within the Finder

Press the space bar

The contents of the file are displayed without it opening in its default program

Hot tip

In Quick Look it is even possible to preview videos or presentations without having to first open them in their default app.

Click on the cross to close Quick Look

Finder Toolbar

Customizing the toolbar

As with most elements of macOS, it is possible to customize the Finder toolbar. To do this:

 Select **View** > **Customize Toolbar...** from the Menu bar

View	Go	Window	Help
as Icons			⌘1
as List			⌘2
✓ as Columns			⌘3
as Cover Flow			⌘4
Clean Up Selection			
Clean Up By			▶
Arrange By			▶
Hide Tab Bar			⇧⌘T
Show Path Bar			⌥⌘P
Show Status Bar			⌘/
Hide Sidebar			⌥⌘S
Hide Preview			⇧⌘P
Hide Toolbar			⌥⌘T
Customize Toolbar...			
Show View Options			⌘J
Enter Full Screen			^⌘F

Beware

Do not put too many items on the Finder toolbar, because you may not be able to see them all in the Finder window. If there are additional toolbar items, there will be a directional arrow indicating this. Click on the arrow to view the available items.

② Drag items from the window into the toolbar

Drag your favorite items into the toolbar...

Back	Path	Arrange	View	Action	Eject	Burn	Space	Flexible Space

New Folder	Delete	Connect	Get Info	Search	Quick Look	Share	Edit Tags

③ Alternatively, drag the default set of icons into the toolbar

... or drag the default set into the toolbar.

Back		View		Arrange	Action	Share	Edit Tags	Search

④ Click **Done** at the bottom of the window

Finder Sidebar

Using the sidebar

The sidebar is the left-hand panel of the Finder which can be used to access items on your Mac. To use this:

1 Click on a button on the sidebar

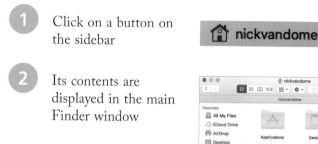

2 Its contents are displayed in the main Finder window

Adding to the sidebar

Items that you access most frequently can be added to the sidebar. To do this:

1 Drag an item from the main Finder window onto the sidebar

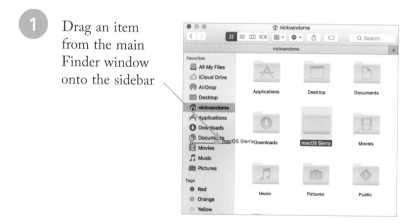

2 A line appears determining the location, and the item is added to the sidebar. You can do this with apps, folders and files

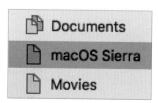

When you click on an item in the sidebar, its contents are shown in the main Finder window to the right.

When items are added to the Finder sidebar, a shortcut, or alias, is inserted into the sidebar, not the actual item.

Items can be removed from the sidebar by Ctrl + clicking on them and selecting **Remove from Sidebar** from the contextual menu.

Finder Search

Searching electronic data is now a massive industry, with companies such as Google leading the way with online searching. On Macs it is also possible to search your folders and files, using the built-in search facilities: the Finder Search, Siri (see pages 18-21) or the Spotlight app (see page 17).

Using Finder

To search for items within the Finder:

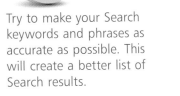

Try to make your Search keywords and phrases as accurate as possible. This will create a better list of Search results.

1 In the Finder window, enter the Search keyword(s) in this box. Search options are listed below the keyword

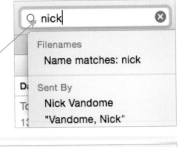

2 Select an option for which category you want to search over

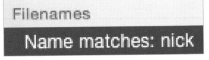

3 The Search results are shown in the Finder window. Click on one of these buttons to search specific areas

Both folders and files will be displayed in the Finder as part of the Search results.

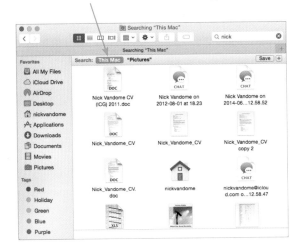

4 Double-click on an item to open it

Copying and Moving Items

Items can be copied and moved within macOS by using the copy and paste method or by dragging.

Copy and paste

1 Select an item (or items) and select **Edit > Copy** from the Menu bar

When an item is copied, it is placed on the Clipboard and remains there until another item is copied.

2 Move to the target location and select **Edit > Paste Item**(s) from the Menu bar. The item is then pasted into the new location

macOS Sierra supports the new Universal Clipboard, where items can be copied on a device such as an iPhone and then pasted directly into a document on a Mac running macOS Sierra. The mobile device has to be running iOS 10 and the Mac has to support the Universal Clipboard. The process is the same as regular copy and paste, except that each operation is performed on the separate device and each app used has to be set up for iCloud. Also, Bluetooth and Wi-Fi have to be activated on both devices.

Dragging

Drag a file from one location to another to move it to that location. (This requires two or more Finder windows to be open, or drag the item over a folder on the sidebar.)

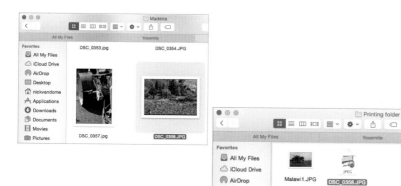

Working with Folders

When macOS Sierra is installed, there are various folders that have already been created to hold apps and files. Some of these are essential (i.e. those containing apps), while others are created as an aid for where you might want to store the files that you create (such as the Pictures and Movies folders). Once you start working with macOS Sierra, you will probably want to create your own folders in which to store and organize your documents. This can be done on the Desktop or within any level of your existing folder structure. To create a new folder:

1 Access the location in which you want to create the new folder (e.g. your Home folder) and select **File > New Folder** from the Menu bar

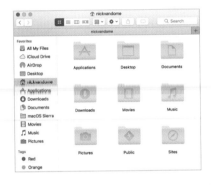

2 A new, empty folder is inserted at the selected location (named "untitled folder")

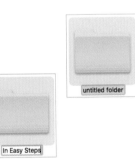

untitled folder

3 Overtype the file name with a new one. Press **Enter**

In Easy Steps

4 Double-click on the folder to view its contents (at this point it should be empty)

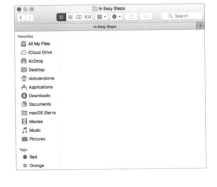

Selecting Items

Apps and files within macOS folders can be selected by a variety of different methods.

Selecting by dragging

Click and drag the cursor to encompass the items to be selected. The selected items will become highlighted.

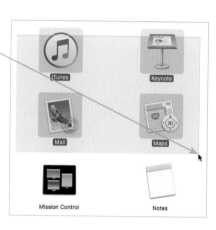

Once items have been selected, a single command can be applied to all of them. For instance, you can copy a group of items by selecting them and then applying the **Copy** command from the Menu bar.

Selecting by clicking

Click once on an item to select it, hold down Shift and then click on another item in a list to select a consecutive group of items.

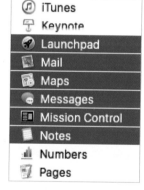

To select a non-consecutive group, select the first item by clicking on it once, then hold down the Command key (**cmd ⌘**) and select the other required items. The selected items will appear highlighted.

To select all of the items in a folder, select **Edit** > **Select All** from the Menu bar. The Select All command selects all of the elements within the active item. For instance, if the active item is a word processing document, the Select All command will select all of the items within the document; if it is a folder, it will select all of the items within that folder. You can also click **cmd** + **A** to select all items.

Finder Tabs

Tabs in web browsers are now well established, and allow you to have several pages open within the same browser window. This technology is now included in the Finder in macOS Sierra with Finder Tabs. This enables different folders to be open in different tabs within the Finder, so that you can organize your content exactly how you want. To do this:

Hot tip

In macOS Sierra, tabs are available in a range of apps that open multiple windows, including the Apple productivity apps: Pages, Numbers and Keynote. If the tabs are not showing, select **View** > **Show Tab Bar** from the app's Menu bar.

Don't forget

To specify an option for what appears in the default window for a new Finder window tab, click on the **Finder** menu and click on **Preferences**, then the **General** tab. Under **New Finder windows show**, select the default window to be used.

1. Select **View** > **Show Tab Bar** from the Finder menu

2. A new tab appears at the right-hand side of the Finder

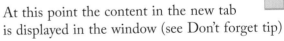

3. Click on this button to open the new tab

4. At this point the content in the new tab is displayed in the window (see Don't forget tip)

5 Access a new folder to display this as the content for the tab. In this way, you can use different tabs for different types of content, such as photos or music, or for different topics such as Work, Travel or Finance within Documents

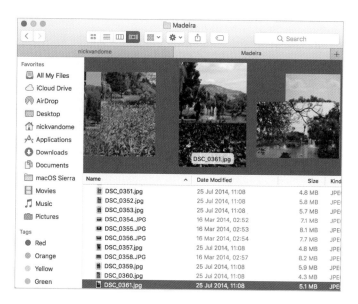

Beware

Dozens of tabs can be added in the Finder. However, when there are too many to fit along the Tab Bar they are stacked on top of each other, so it can be hard to work out what you have in your tabs.

6 Each tab view can be customized and this is independent of the other tabs

Tagging in the Finder

When creating content in macOS Sierra, you may find that you have documents of different types that cover the same topic. For instance, you may have work-related documents in Pages for reports, Keynote for presentations and Numbers for spreadsheets. With the Finder Tags function it is possible to link items with related content through the use of colored tags. These can be added to items in the Finder and also in apps when content is created.

Hot tip

Tags can also be added to items by Ctrl + clicking on them and selecting the required tag from the context menu that appears. Also, they can be added from this button on the main Finder toolbar.

Hot tip

Tags can be dragged onto the Dock so that all items with a specific tag can be accessed from here. To do this, drag the tag from the Finder sidebar to the right-hand side of the Dock's dividing line. This will create a Stack containing all of the items with the selected tag.

1. The tags are listed in the Finder sidebar. (If you can't see the list, hover the cursor over the Tags heading and then click the **Show** button)

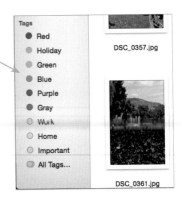

2. To give tags specific names, Ctrl + click on one and click on the **Rename** option

3. To add tags, select the required items in the Finder window

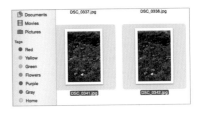

4. Drag the selected items over the appropriate tag

5 The tags are added to the selected items

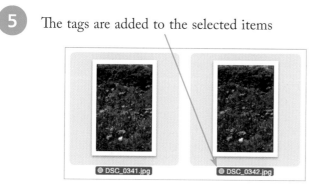

Adding tags in apps

Tags can also be added when documents are created in certain apps, such as Pages, Keynote and Numbers.

1 Select **File** > **Save**, click in the **Tags** box and select the required tag. Click on the **Save** button

73

Hot tip

Tags can also be added to iCloud documents so that when you are viewing content in iCloud, all tagged items can be viewed together.

Viewing tags

To view all documents that have had the same tag added:

1 Click on the required tag in the Finder sidebar. All of the tagged documents will be displayed, regardless of their content type, or where they are saved on your Mac

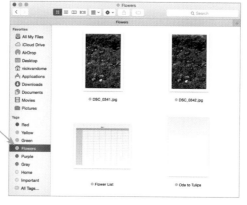

Spring-loaded Folders

Another method for moving items with the Finder is to use the spring-loaded folder option. This enables you to drag items over a folder and then view the contents of the folder before you drop the item into it. This means that you can drag items into nested folders in a single operation. To do this:

1 Select the item you want to move

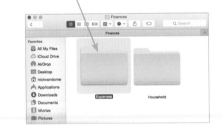

2 Drag the selected item over the folder into which you want to place it. Keep the mouse held down

3 The folder will open, revealing its contents. The selected item can either be dropped into the folder or, if there are sub-folders, the same operation can be repeated until you find the folder into which you want to place the selected item. Release the item to complete the operation

Burnable Folders

With the increasing use of images, digital video and music files, computer users are often copying data from their computers onto CDs. In some cases this can be a frustrating process, but in macOS Sierra the use of burnable folders can make the process much quicker. These are folders that can be created specifically for the contents to be burned onto a CD or DVD. To do this:

Only Macs with a SuperDrive can burn CDs and DVDs. If there is not an internal one, an external one can be used instead.

 In the Finder, select **File** > **New Burn Folder** from the Menu bar

The burn folder is created in the Finder window which was active when Step 1 was performed. Click on the folder name and overtype to give it a unique name

Select the items that you want to burn, and drag and drop or copy and paste them into the burn folder

Applications such as iTunes can be used to burn CDs using the content within that application, but burnable folders are the best way to combine files from a variety of different applications and then burn them onto discs.

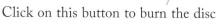

Click on this button to burn the disc

Actions Button

The Finder Actions button provides a variety of options for any item, or items, selected in the Finder. To use this:

The icons on the Finder toolbar can be changed by customizing them – see page 64.

1 Select an item, or group of items, about which you want to find out additional information

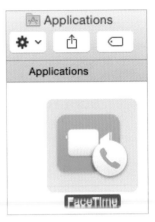

The Actions button can also be used for labeling items with Finder Tags. To do this, select the required items in the Finder and click one of the colored dots at the bottom of the Actions button menu. The selected tag will be applied to the item names in the Finder.

2 Click on the **Actions** button on the Finder toolbar

3 The available options for the selected item, or items, are displayed. These include **Get Info** which displays additional information about an item, such as file type, file size, creation and modification dates, and the default app for opening the item(s)

New Folder
Open
Show Package Contents

Move to Trash

Get Info
Compress "FaceTime"
Burn "FaceTime" to Disc...
Duplicate
Make Alias
Quick Look "FaceTime"

Copy "FaceTime"
Paste 5 Items

Arrange By ▶
Show View Options

Add to Evernote
Reveal in Finder

Sharing from the Finder

Also on the Finder toolbar is the Share button. This can be used to share a selected item, or items, in a variety of ways appropriate to the type of file that has been selected. For instance, a photo will have options including the photo sharing site Flickr, while a text document will have fewer options. To share items directly from the Finder:

1. Locate and select the item(s) that you want to share

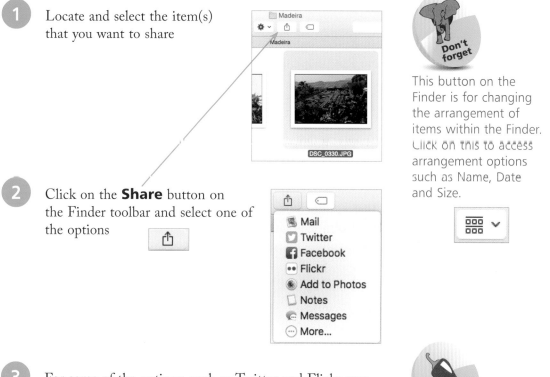

2. Click on the **Share** button on the Finder toolbar and select one of the options

3. For some of the options, such as Twitter and Flickr, you will be asked to add an account. If you already have an account with these services you can enter the details or, if not, you can create a new account

77

This button on the Finder is for changing the arrangement of items within the Finder. Click on this to access arrangement options such as Name, Date and Size.

You can also add your social networking accounts from **System Preferences** > **Internet Accounts**. Select the required account and enter your log in details.

Menus

The main Apple Menu bar in macOS Sierra contains a variety of menus, which are accessed when the Finder is the active window. When individual apps are open they have their own Menu bars, although in a lot of cases these are similar to the standard Menu bar, particularly for the built-in macOS Sierra apps such as Calendar, Contacts and Notes.

- **Apple menu**. This is denoted by a translucent blue apple and contains general information about the computer, links to the System Preferences and the App Store for app updates, and options for closing down your Mac.

- **Finder menu**. This contains preference options for amending the functionality and appearance of the Finder, and also options for emptying the Trash and accessing other apps (under the Services option).

- **File menu**. This contains common commands for working with open documents, such as opening and closing files, creating aliases, moving to the Trash, ejecting external devices and burning discs.

- **Edit menu**. This contains common commands that apply to the majority of apps used on the Mac. These include Undo, Cut, Copy, Paste, Select All and Show the contents of the Clipboard, i.e. items that have been cut or copied.

- **View menu**. This contains options for how windows and folders are displayed within the Finder, and for customizing the Finder toolbar. This includes showing or hiding the Finder sidebar and selecting view options for the size at which icons are displayed within Finder windows.

- **Go menu**. This can be used to navigate around your computer. This includes moving to your All My Files folder, your Home folder, your Applications folder and recently accessed folders.

- **Window menu**. This contains commands to organize the currently open apps and files on your Desktop.

- **Help menu**. This contains the Mac Help files which contain information about all aspects of macOS Sierra.

4 Navigating in macOS Sierra

macOS Sierra has
Multi–Touch gestures for
navigating around your apps
and documents. This chapter
looks at how to use these to
get around your Mac and
also using Mission Control.

80 The macOS Way of Navigating

81 macOS Scroll Bars

82 Split View

84 Trackpad Gestures

92 Magic Mouse Gestures

95 Multi-Touch Preferences

97 Mission Control

98 Spaces

The macOS Way of Navigating

One of the most revolutionary features of earlier versions of OS X, which is continued with macOS Sierra, is the way in which you can navigate around your applications, web pages and documents. This involves a much greater reliance on swiping on a trackpad or adapted mouse; techniques that have been imported from the iPhone and the iPad. These are known as Multi-Touch Gestures and to take full advantage of these you will need to have one of the following devices:

- **A trackpad**. This can be found on MacBooks.

- **A Magic Trackpad**. This can be used with an iMac, a Mac Mini or a Mac Pro. It works wirelessly via Bluetooth.

- **A Magic Mouse**. This can be used with an iMac, a Mac Mini or a Mac Pro. It works wirelessly via Bluetooth.

All of these devices work using a swiping technique with fingers moving over their surface. This should be done with a light touch; it is a gentle swipe, rather than any pressure being applied to the device.

The trackpads and Magic Mouse do not have any buttons in the same way as traditional devices. Instead, specific areas are clickable so that you can still perform left- and right-click operations.

On a Magic Mouse, the center and right side can be used for clicking operations, and on a Magic Trackpad, the left and right corners can perform the same tasks.

Models of MacBooks from May 2015 onwards, (and the Magic Trackpad 2) employ a technology known as Force Touch. This provides the user with different options, depending on how firmly they press on the trackpad. This means that more than one function can be performed, simply by pressing more firmly on the trackpad. It also provides haptic feedback, which is a physical response from the trackpad in the form of a small vibration, once different options have been accessed.

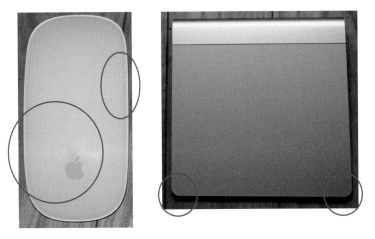

macOS Scroll Bars

In macOS Sierra, scroll bars in web pages and documents are more reactive to the navigational device being used on the computer. By default, with a Magic Trackpad, a trackpad or a Magic Mouse, scroll bars are only visible when scrolling is actually taking place. However, if a mouse is being used they will be visible permanently, although this can be changed for all devices.
To perform scrolling with macOS Sierra:

1 Scroll around a web page or document by swiping up or down on a Magic Mouse, a Magic Trackpad, or a trackpad. As you move up or down, the scroll bar appears

2 When you stop scrolling, the bar disappears to allow optimum viewing area for your web page or document

3 To change the scroll bar options, select **System Preferences** > **General** and select the required settings under **Show scroll bars**

If you do not have a trackpad, a Magic Trackpad or a Magic Mouse you can still navigate in macOS Sierra with a traditional mouse and the use of scroll bars in windows.

For instructions on scrolling with a Magic Mouse, see page 93. For scrolling with a Magic Trackpad, see pages 86-87.

Split View

When working with computers it can sometimes be beneficial to be able to view two windows next to each other. This can be to compare information in two different windows, or just to be able to use two windows without having to access them from the Desktop each time. In macOS Sierra, two windows can be displayed next to each other using the Split View feature:

 By default, all open windows are layered on top of each other, with the active one at the top

Don't forget

If you click once on the green maximize button this will display the app in full screen mode, rather than holding on it to activate Split View.

 Press and hold on the green maximize button to activate Split View. The active window is displayed on the left-hand side of the screen, with thumbnails of the other open apps on the right-hand side

3 Click on one of the apps on the right-hand side in Step 2 to add it as the other Split View panel. Click on each window in Split View to make it active

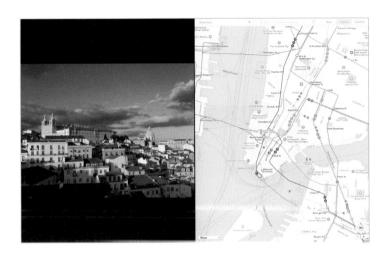

You can work in one panel in Split View, i.e. move through web pages, without affecting the content of the app on the other side.

4 Drag the middle divider bar to resize either of the Split View panels, to change the viewing area

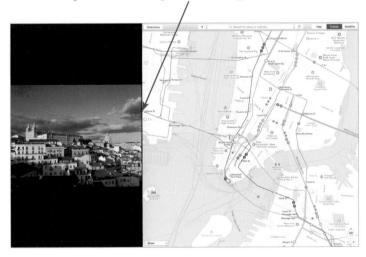

Swap the windows in Split View by dragging the top toolbar of one app into the other window.

5 Move the cursor over the top of the window of each Split View item to view its toolbar and controls

Trackpad Gestures

Pointing and clicking

A Magic Trackpad, or trackpad, can be used to perform a variety of pointing and clicking tasks:

By default, the iMac with Retina Display comes with a Magic Mouse provided. However, this can be swapped for a Magic Trackpad, or both can be included for an additional cost.

 Tap with one finger in the middle of the Magic Trackpad or trackpad, to perform a single click operation, e.g. to click on a button or click on an open window

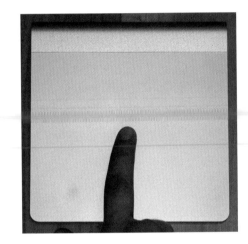

 Tap once with two fingers in the middle of the Magic Trackpad or trackpad, to access any contextual menus associated with an item (this is the equivalent of the traditional right-click with a mouse)

3 Highlight a word or phrase and double-tap with three fingers to see look-up information for the selected item. This is frequently a dictionary definition but it can also be a Wikipedia entry

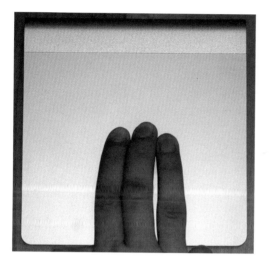

 4 Move over an item and drag with three fingers to move the item around the screen

Beware

If you have too many functions set using the same number of fingers, some of them may not work. See pages 95-96 for details about setting preferences for Multi-Touch Gestures.

...cont'd

Scrolling and zooming

One of the most common operations on a computer is scrolling on a page, whether it is a web page or a document. Traditionally, this has been done with a mouse and a cursor. However, using a Magic Trackpad you can now do all of your scrolling with your fingers. There are a number of options for doing this.

Scrolling up and down

To move up and down web pages or documents, use two fingers on the Magic Trackpad or trackpad, and swipe up or down. The page moves in the opposite direction to the one in which you are swiping, i.e. if you swipe up, the page moves down and vice versa.

Don't forget

Don't worry if you cannot immediately get the hang of Multi-Touch Gestures. It takes a bit of practice to get the correct touch and pressure on the Magic Trackpad, trackpad or Magic Mouse.

 Open a web page

 Position two fingers in the middle of the Magic Trackpad or trackpad

3 Swipe them up to move down the page

4 Swipe them down to move up a page

...cont'd

Zooming in and out
To zoom in or out on web pages or documents:

 To zoom in, position your thumb and forefinger in the middle of the Magic Trackpad or trackpad

Pages can also be zoomed in on by double-tapping with two fingers.

 Spread them outwards to zoom in on a web page or document

3 To zoom out, position your thumb and forefinger at opposite corners of the Magic Trackpad or trackpad

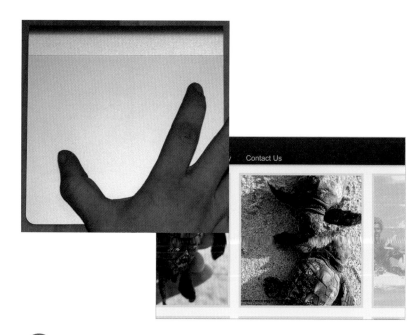

Don't forget

There is a limit on how far you can zoom in or out on a web page or document, to ensure that it does not distort the content too much.

4 Pinch them into the center of the Magic Trackpad or trackpad, to zoom out

...cont'd

Moving between pages

With Multi-Touch Gestures, it is possible to swipe between pages within a document. To do this:

 Position two fingers to the left or right of the Magic Trackpad or trackpad

 Swipe to the opposite side of the Magic Trackpad or trackpad, to move through the document

Don't forget

See pages 102-103 for details about using full screen apps.

Moving between full screen apps

In addition to moving between pages by swiping, it is also possible to move between different apps when they are in full screen mode. To do this:

 Position three fingers to the left or right of the Magic Trackpad or trackpad

Swipe to the opposite side of the Magic Trackpad or trackpad, to move through the available full screen apps

Showing the Desktop

To show the whole Desktop, regardless of how many files or apps are open:

 Position your thumb and three fingers in the middle of the Magic Trackpad or trackpad

 Swipe to the opposite corners of the Magic Trackpad or trackpad, to display the Desktop

 The Desktop is displayed, with all items minimized around the side of the screen

Magic Mouse Gestures

Pointing and clicking

A Magic Mouse can be used to perform a variety of pointing and clicking tasks:

 Click with one finger on the Magic Mouse to perform a single-click operation, e.g. to select a button or command

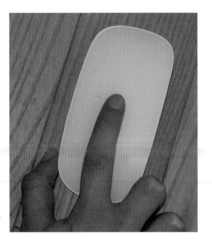

The right-click operation can be set within the Mouse System Preferences.

 Tap with one finger on the right side of the Magic Mouse to access any contextual menus associated with an item (this is the equivalent of the traditional right-click with a mouse)

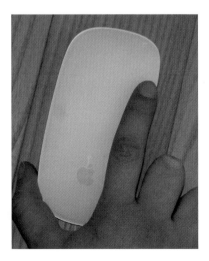

Scrolling and zooming

The Magic Mouse can also be used to perform scrolling and zooming functions within a web page or document:

 Swipe up or down with one finger to move up or down a web page or document

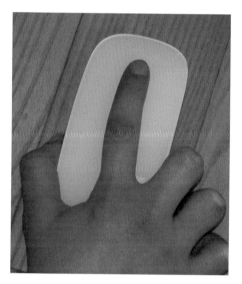

When scrolling on a web page or document, it moves in the opposite direction to the movement of your finger, i.e. if you swipe up, the page moves down and vice versa.

 Double-tap with one finger to zoom in on a web page

...cont'd

 Swipe left or right with one finger to move between pages

 Swipe left or right with two fingers to move between full screen apps

Multi-Touch Preferences

Some Multi-Touch Gestures only have a single action, which cannot be changed. However, others have options for changing the action linked to a specific gesture. This is done within the respective preferences for the Magic Mouse, the Magic Trackpad or the trackpad, where a full list of Multi-Touch Gestures is shown. To use these:

1 Access the System Preferences and click on the **Mouse** or **Trackpad** button

Trackpad

2 Click on one of the tabs at the top

More Gestures

3 The actions are described on the left, with a graphic explanation on the right

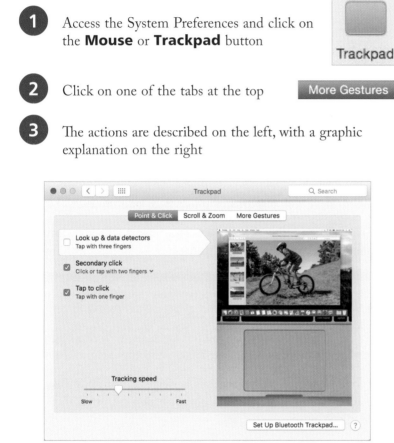

Don't forget

The Magic Trackpad or trackpad, has three tabbed options within the System Preferences: Point & Click, Scroll & Zoom and More Gestures. The Magic Mouse has preferences for Point & Click and More Gestures.

4 If there is a down arrow next to an option, click on it to change the way a gesture is actioned

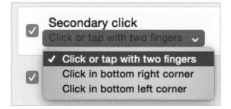

...cont'd

Trackpad gestures

The full list of trackpad Multi-Touch Gestures, with their default action are: (relevant ones for Magic Mouse are in brackets)

Point & Click

- Tap to click – tap once with one finger (same for the Magic Mouse)

- Secondary click – click or tap with two fingers (single-click on the right of the Magic Mouse)

- Look up – double-tap with three fingers

- Three finger drag – move with three fingers

Scroll & Zoom

- Scroll direction: natural – with two fingers, content tracks finger movement (one finger with the Magic Mouse)

- Zoom in or out – spread or pinch with two fingers

- Smart zoom – double-tap with two fingers (double-tap with one finger with the Magic Mouse)

- Rotate – rotate with two fingers

More Gestures

- Swipe between pages – scroll left or right with two fingers (scroll left or right with one finger with the Magic Mouse)

- Swipe between full screen apps – swipe left or right with three fingers (swipe left or right with two fingers with the Magic Mouse)

- Swipe left from the right-hand edge of the trackpad or Magic Trackpad to access the Notification Center

- Access Mission Control (see next page) – swipe up with three fingers (double-tap with two fingers with the Magic Mouse)

- App Exposé – swipe down with three fingers

- Access Launchpad – pinch with thumb and three fingers

- Show Desktop – spread with thumb and three fingers

Don't forget

Natural scrolling means the page follows the direction of your finger, vertically or horizontally, depending on which way you're scrolling.

Hot tip

Exposé enables you to view all of the active windows that are currently open for a particular app.

Mission Control

Mission Control is a function in macOS Sierra that helps you organize all of your open apps, full screen apps and documents. It also enables you to quickly view the Desktop. Within Mission Control there is also Spaces, where you can group similar types of documents together. To use Mission Control:

 1 Click on this button in the Applications folder, or Swipe upwards with three fingers on the Magic Trackpad or trackpad, or double-tap with two fingers on a Magic Mouse

2 All open files and apps are visible via Mission Control

3 If there is more than one window open for an app they will each be shown separately

4 Move the cursor over the top of the Mission Control window to view the different Spaces (see page 98) and any apps in full screen mode

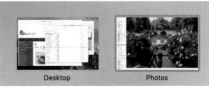

(see page 98)

Click on a window in Mission Control to access it and exit the Mission Control window.

Any apps or files that have been minimized or closed do not appear within the main Mission Control window. Instead, they are located to the right of the dividing line on the Dock.

Drag an open app to the top of the screen to access Mission Control. You can then make an app full screen from Mission Control by dragging it onto one of the Spaces at the top of the window.

Spaces

The top level of Mission Control contains Spaces, which are new Desktop areas into which you can group certain apps, e.g. the iWork apps such as Pages and Numbers. This means that you can access these apps independently from every other open item. This helps to organize your apps and files. To use Spaces:

Don't forget

Preferences for Spaces can be set within the Mission Control System Preference.

1 Move the cursor over the top right-hand corner of Mission Control and click on the **+** symbol

Hot tip

Create different Spaces for different types of content, e.g. one for productivity and one for entertainment.

2 A new **Space** is created along the top row of Mission Control

Desktop 2

3 Drag an app onto the Space, and then any additional apps required

Desktop 2

Don't forget

When you create a new Space it can subsequently be deleted by moving the cursor over it and clicking on the cross at the left-hand corner. Any items that have been added to this Space are returned to the default Desktop Space.

4 The new Space can then be accessed by clicking on the Space within Mission Control, and all of the apps that have been placed here will be available

Desktop 2

5 macOS Sierra Apps

Apps are the programs with which you can start putting macOS Sierra to use, either for work or for fun. This chapter looks at using apps and the online App Store.

100   Launchpad

102   Full Screen Apps

104   macOS Apps

105   Accessing the App Store

106   Downloading Apps

108   Finding Apps

110   Managing Your Apps

Launchpad

Even though the Dock can be used to store shortcuts to your applications, it is limited in terms of space. The full set of applications on your Mac can be found in the Finder (see Chapter Three) but macOS Sierra has a feature that allows you to quickly access and manage all of your applications. These include the ones that are pre-installed on your Mac and also any that you install yourself or download from the Apple App Store. This feature is called Launchpad. To use it:

Hot tip

If the apps take up more than one screen, swipe from right to left with two fingers to view the additional pages, or click on the white dots at the bottom of the window.

1 Click once on this button on the Dock

2 All of the apps (applications) are displayed

Don't forget

To launch an app from within Launchpad, click it once.

Hot tip

One of the apps in Utilities is Boot Camp Assistant, which can be used to run Windows on your Mac, if required.

3 Similar types of apps can be grouped together in individual folders. By default, the **Utilities** are grouped in this way

4 To create a group of similar apps, drag the icon for one over another

5 The apps are grouped together in a folder and Launchpad gives it a name, based on the types of apps within the folder, usually the one into which the selected app is placed

6 To change the name, click on it once and overtype it with the new name

Don't forget

System apps, i.e. the ones that already come with your Mac, cannot be removed in the Launchpad, only ones you have downloaded.

7 The folder appears within the **Launchpad** window

8 To remove an app, click and hold on it until it starts to jiggle and a cross appears. Click on the cross to remove it

Full Screen Apps

When working with apps we all like to be able to see as much of the selected window as possible. With macOS Sierra this is possible with the full screen option. This allows you to expand an app with this functionality so that it takes up the whole of your monitor or screen with a minimum of toolbars visible. Some apps have this functionality but some do not. To use full screen with apps:

 By default, an app appears on the Desktop with other windows behind it

If the button in Step 2 is not visible then the app does not have the full screen functionality.

 Click on this button at the top left-hand corner of the app's window

The app is expanded to take up the whole window. The main Apple Menu bar and the Dock are hidden

4 To view the main Menu bar, move the cursor over the top of the screen

| **🍎** | **App Store** | Edit | Store | Window | Help |

5 You can move between all full screen apps by swiping with three fingers left or right on a trackpad or Magic Mouse

Hot tip

For more information about navigating with Multi-Touch Gestures see pages 84-96.

6 Move the cursor over the top left-hand corner of the screen and click on this button to close the full screen functionality

7 In Mission Control, all of the open full screen apps are shown in the top row

Desktop 1   Maps   Photos

macOS Apps

macOS Sierra apps include:

- **Automator**. An app for creating automated processes

- **Calculator**. A basic calculator

- **Calendar**. (See pages 114-115)

- **Contacts**. (See pages 112-113)

- **Dashboard**. A range of widgets to use on your Mac

- **Dictionary**. A digital dictionary

- **DVD Player**. Used to play and view DVDs

- **FaceTime**. Can be used for video calls (see page 144)

- **Font Book**. Use this to add and change fonts

- **iBooks**. An app for downloading ebooks (see pages 155-156)

- **iTunes, Photos, iMovie, and GarageBand**.
  (See Chapter Eight for details about iTunes and the Photos app, which supersedes iPhoto.)

- **Mail**. The default email app

- **Maps**. For viewing locations and destinations worldwide

- **Messages**. (See pages 142-143)

- **Mission Control**. The function for organizing your Desktop

- **Notes**. (See pages 116-117)

- **Photo Booth**. An app for creating photo effects

- **Preview**. (See page 126)

- **QuickTime Player**. Apple's own app for viewing video

- **Reminders**. (See pages 118-119)

- **Safari**. The macOS specific web browser

- **TextEdit**. An app for editing text files

- **Time Machine**. macOS's backup facility

The macOS apps can be accessed from the Launchpad and also from the Applications folder within the Finder.

There are not many games apps with macOS, but the Chess app is one of those available.

For qualifying Macs with macOS Sierra, the iWork apps (Pages, Numbers and Keynote) are free to download from the App Store, or come pre-installed.

Several apps are available in the App Store for watching YouTube videos. This can also be done from the YouTube website using Safari.

Accessing the App Store

Another macOS app is the App Store. This is an online facility where you can buy and download new apps. These cover a range of categories such as productivity, business and entertainment. When you get or buy an app from the App Store, it is downloaded automatically by Launchpad and appears there next to the rest of the apps.

To get or buy apps from the App Store you need to have an Apple ID (even if the app you wish to get is free). If you have not already set this up, it can be done when you first access the App Store. To use the App Store:

The App Store is an online function so you need an internet connection to access it.

 Click on this icon on the Dock or within the Launchpad

 The Homepage of the App Store contains the current top featured and best new apps

You can set up an Apple ID when you first set up your Mac or you can do it when you register for the App Store or the iTunes Store. You can also visit **https://appleid. apple.com**, click the **Create your Apple ID** link, and follow the instructions.

 Your account information and quick link categories are listed at the right-hand side of the page

Quick Links

Welcome
Account
Redeem
Support

macOS Sierra
Apps Made by Apple
New to the Mac App Store?
Great Free Apps & Games
Editors' Choice

Downloading Apps

The App Store contains a wide range of apps: from small, fun apps, to powerful productivity ones. However, downloading them from the App Store is the same regardless of the type of app. The only differences are whether they need to be paid for or not and the length of time they take to download. To download an app from the App Store:

1 Browse through the App Store until you find the required app

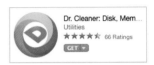

2 Click on the app to view a detailed description about it

Hot tip

When downloading apps, start with a free one first so that you can get used to the process before you download paid-for apps.

3 Click on the button underneath the app icon to download it. If there is no charge for the app the button will say **Get**

4 If there is a charge for the app, the button will say **Buy App**

5 Click on the **Install App** button

6 Enter your **Apple ID** account details to continue downloading the app

Don't forget

Depending on their sizes, different apps take differing amounts of time to be downloaded.

7 The progress of the download is displayed in a progress bar underneath the Launchpad icon on the Dock

8 Once it has been downloaded, the app is available within the Launchpad

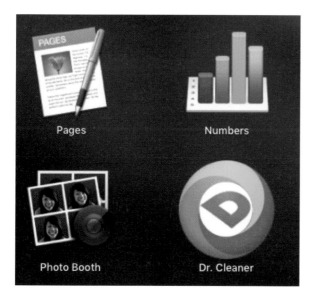

Don't forget

As you download more apps, additional pages will be created within the Launchpad to accommodate them.

Finding Apps

There are thousands of apps in the App Store, and sometimes the hardest task is locating the ones you want. However, there are a number of ways in which finding apps is made as easy as possible:

 Click on the **Featured** button

 The main window has a range of categories such as New Apps & Games We Love and Our Favorite Mac Apps. At the right-hand side there is a panel with the current top **Paid** apps

Paid   See All >

1. **GarageBand**
   Music

2. **The Sims™ 2: Super Collection**
   Games

3. **Logic Pro X**
   Music

4. **App for WhatsApp**
   Social Networking

 Underneath this is a list of the current top **Free** apps

Free   See All >

1. **Microsoft Remote Desktop**
   Business

2. **OneDrive**
   Productivity

3. **Word Document Writer for Mi...**
   Business

4. **FreeChat for WhatsApp**
   Social Networking

...cont'd

 Click on the **Top Charts** button

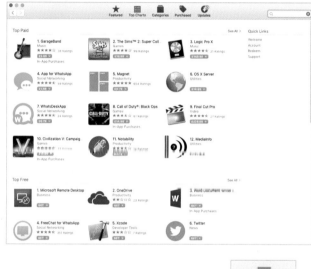 The top apps for different categories are displayed

The Top Charts has sections for paid-for apps and free ones.

Click on the **Categories** button

Categories

Browse through the apps by specific categories, such as Business, Entertainment and Finance

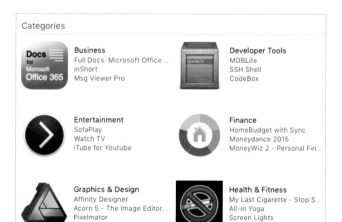

Managing Your Apps

Once you have bought apps from the App Store, you can view details of ones you have purchased and also install updated versions of them.

Purchased apps

To view your purchased apps:

Even if you interrupt a download and turn off your Mac, you will still be able to resume the download when you next start your computer.

  Click on the **Purchased** button

 Details of your purchased apps are displayed (including those that are free)

If a download of an app has been interrupted, click on the **Resume** button to continue downloading it.

Updating apps

Improvements and fixes to apps are being developed constantly, and these can be downloaded to ensure that all of your apps are up-to-date:

Apps can also be updated automatically. This can be specified in **System Preferences > App Store**. Check **On** the **Automatically check for updates** option. Underneath this there are options for downloading and installing updates.

 When updates are available, this is indicated by a red, numbered circle on the App Store icon in the Dock, in the same way as you would be alerted to new emails

 Click on the **Updates** button

 Information about the update is displayed next to the app that is due to be updated

Click on the **Update** button to update an individual app

UPDATE

Click on the **Update All** button to update all of the apps that are due to be updated

UPDATE ALL

6 Getting Productive

There are several built-in apps within macOS Sierra that can be used to create, store and display information. This chapter shows how to access and use these apps, so that you can get the most out of macOS Sierra as a productivity tool.

112 Contacts (Address Book)

114 Calendar

116 Taking Notes

118 Setting Reminders

120 Notifications

122 Getting Around with Maps

126 Preview

127 Printing

128 macOS Utilities

130 Creating PDF Documents

Contacts (Address Book)

The Contacts app can be used to store contact information, which can then be used in different apps and shared via iCloud. To view contacts:

Contacts can be shared by clicking on the **Share** button and selecting one of the available options.

1 Open **Contacts** from this address book icon, and click on one in the left-hand panel to view their details

Adding contact information

The main function of the Contacts app is to store details of personal and business contacts. Contacts must be added manually for each entry, but it can prove to be a valuable resource once this has been completed. To add contact information:

Hot tip

Click on this button to add a new contact, rather than editing an existing one.

1 Click on the **Edit** button to edit contacts   Edit

2 Click on a category and enter contact information. Press the **Tab** key to move to the next field

3 Click on the **Done** button once you have edited the entry

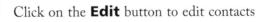

Creating groups

In addition to creating individual entries in the Contacts app, group contacts can also be created. This is a way of grouping contacts with similar interests or connections. Once a group has been created, all of the entries within it can be accessed and contacted by selecting the relevant entry in the left-hand panel. To create a group:

Don't forget

Individuals can be included in several groups. If you change their details in one group, these changes will take effect across all of the groups in which the entry occurs.

 Select **File** > **New Group** from the Menu bar to create a new group entry

2 Give the new group a name

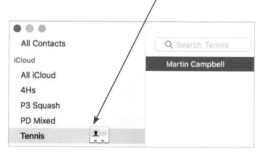

3 Drag individual entries into the group (the individual entries are retained too)

Hot tip

Groups in the Contacts app can be used to send group emails, i.e. you can type the name of the group into the **Mail To** box to generate the names in the group, and then send the email to all of these recipients.

4 Click on a group name to view the members of the group

113

Calendar

Electronic calendars are now a standard part of modern life, and with macOS this function is performed by the Calendar app. Not only can this be used on your Mac, it can also be synchronized with other Apple devices such as an iPod or an iPhone, using iCloud. To create a calendar:

Hot tip

The Calendar app displays the current date in the icon on the Dock.

1 Click on this icon on the Dock, or in the Launchpad

2 Select whether to view the calendar by Day, Week, Month or Year

Day	Week	**Month**	Year

Don't forget

Click on the **Today** button to view the current day. Click on the forward or back arrows to move to the next day, week, month or year, depending on what is selected in Step 2.

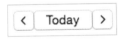

3 In Month view, the current day is denoted by a red circle on the date

Hot tip

If Family Sharing has been activated, the Family calendar will automatically be added, for all members of the Family Sharing group.

4 Scroll up and down to move through the weeks and months. In macOS Sierra this is done with continuous scrolling, which means you can view weeks across different months, rather than just viewing each month in its entirety, i.e. you can view the second half of one month and the first half of the next one in the same window

Adding events

1 Select a date and double-click on it, or Ctrl + click on the date, then select **New Event**

2 Click on the **New Event** field and enter an event name

3 Click on the date or time to amend it by entering new details. Check on the all-day box to set the event for a whole day

Click on this button to add a **Quick Event**, with just one text box for all of the relevant information. Once it has been added it can then be edited like a regular event by double-clicking on it.

Finding locations
When adding events you can also find details about locations:

1 Click on the **Add Location** field and start typing a destination name or zip (postal) code. Suggestions will appear underneath, including matching items from your contacts list. Click on a location to select it

2 A map of the location is displayed, including a real-time weather summary for the location. Click on the map to view it in greater detail in the **Maps** app

Other items that can be included in an event are: inviting people to it, calculating the travel time from your current location, creating a repeat event and setting an alert for it.

Taking Notes

It is always useful to have a quick way of making notes of everyday things, such as shopping lists, recipes or packing lists for traveling. With macOS Sierra, the Notes app is perfect for this task. To use it:

1 Click on this icon on the Dock, or in the Launchpad

2 The right-hand panel is where the note is created. The middle panel displays a list of all notes

3 Click on this button to show or hide the left-hand panel in the Notes app, which displays the notes folders

4 Click on this button to add a new note

5 As more notes are added, the most recent appears at the top of the list in the middle panel. Double click the new note to add text and edit formatting options (see next page)

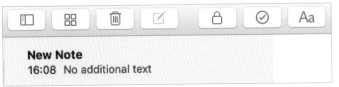

Formatting notes

In macOS Sierra there are a number of formatting options for the Notes app:

1 Enter a line of text and click on this button to add a check button

2 Click on the check button to add a tick, to indicate that an item has been completed

3 Highlight a piece of text and click on this button to access formatting options for it

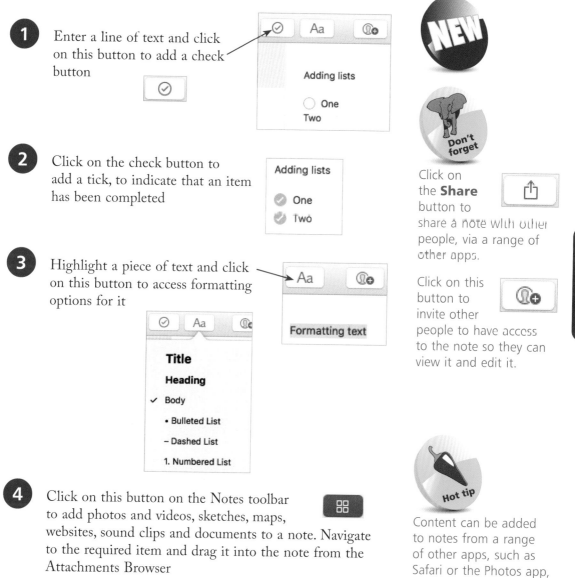

4 Click on this button on the Notes toolbar to add photos and videos, sketches, maps, websites, sound clips and documents to a note. Navigate to the required item and drag it into the note from the Attachments Browser

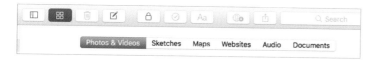

NEW

Don't forget

Click on the **Share** button to share a note with other people, via a range of other apps.

Click on this button to invite other people to have access to the note so they can view it and edit it.

Hot tip

Content can be added to notes from a range of other apps, such as Safari or the Photos app, by clicking on the **Share** button in the relevant app and selecting **Notes** as the option.

Setting Reminders

Another useful app for keeping organized is Reminders. This enables you to create lists for different topics and also set reminders for specific items. A date and time can be set for each reminder and, when this is reached, the reminder appears on your Mac screen (and in the Notification Center). To use Reminders:

1 Click on this icon on the Dock, or in the Launchpad

2 Lists can be created for different categories of reminders. The Reminder lists are located in the left-hand panel. Click on a list name to add reminders here. Click on **+ Add List** to add a new list

3 Click on this button to add a new reminder, or click on a new line

4 Enter text for the reminder

5 Click on this button to change settings for the reminder

Don't forget

As with Notes, iCloud makes your reminders available on all of your Apple devices, i.e. your Mac, iPad, iPhone and iPod Touch.

Hot tip

Hover over a reminder name to access the 'i' symbol.

6 Check on this button to add a time and date for the reminder

Renew passport

remind me ☑ On a Day
17/08/2016 17:00
☐ At a Location
repeat None
priority None
note None

Done

7 Click on the date and select a date for when you want the reminder alert. Do the same for the time, by typing a new time over the one showing

Renew passport

remind me ☑ On a Day
17/08/2016 17:00

Aug 2016 ◀ • ▶
Mo Tu We Th Fr Sa Su
1 2 3 4 5 6 7
8 9 10 11 12 13 14
15 16 **17** 18 19 20 21
22 23 24 25 26 27 28
29 30 31 1 2 3 4

Done

8 If required, add details for a repeat reminder and a priority level

repeat None

priority None
note None

9 Click on the **Done** button

Done

Hot tip

For a recurring reminder, click on the text next to **repeat**, visible in Step 6, and select a repeat option from **None, Every Day, Every Week, Every Month** or **Every Year** or **Custom...**.

119

10 The reminder is set for the specified date and time. This will appear on the screen when the time arrives, and also in Notifications if it is set up for Reminders (see pages 120-121)

Reminders +
64 Completed Show
○ Renew passport ⓘ

11 Check on this button to move a reminder to the Completed list

Reminders +
64 Completed Show
◉ Renew passport
Today 17:00

Notifications

The Notification Center provides a single location to view all of your emails, messages, updates and alerts. Notifications appear at the top right-hand corner of the screen. The items that appear in Notifications are set up within System Preferences. To do this:

Notifications can be accessed regardless of the app in which you are working, and they can be actioned directly without having to leave the active app.

Twitter and Facebook feeds can also be set up to appear in the Notification Center, if you have accounts with these sites.

 1 Open System Preferences and click on the **Notifications** button

Notifications

2 The items that will appear in the Notification Center are listed here. Click on an item to select it and set its notification options

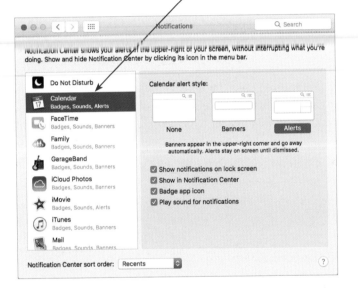

3 To disable an item so that it does not appear in the Notification Center, select it as above and check **Off** the **Show in Notification Center** box

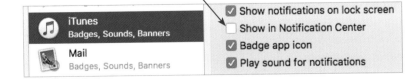

Viewing notifications

Notifications appear in the Notification Center. The way they appear can be determined in System Preferences:

 Select an alert style. A banner alert comes up on the screen and then disappears after a few seconds

2 The **Alerts** option shows the notification and it stays on screen until dismissed (such as this one for reminders)

3 Click on this button in the top right-hand corner of the screen to view all of the items in the Notification Center. Click on it again to hide the Notification Center

4 In the Notification Center, click on the **Today** button to view the weather forecast, calendar events and stock market reports for the current day. Click on the **Edit** button at the bottom to change the items that appear

5 Click on the **Notifications** button to view the items that have been set up to appear here. Items such as emails and iMessages can be replied to directly by clicking on them from within the Notifications section

Hot tip

The Notification Center can also be displayed using a trackpad or Magic Trackpad by dragging with two fingers from right to left, starting from the far right edge.

Don't forget

Software updates can also appear in the Notification Center, when they are available.

Getting Around with Maps

With the Maps app you need never again wonder about where a location is, or worry about getting directions to somewhere. Using Maps with macOS Sierra, you will be able to do the following:

- Search maps from around the world
- Find addresses
- Find famous buildings or landmarks
- Get directions between different locations
- View transit information for a route
- View traffic conditions

Viewing maps

Enable **Location Services** and then you can start looking around maps, from the viewpoint of your current location.

Location Services can be enabled in **System Preferences > Security & Privacy**. Click on the **Privacy** tab, click on **Location Services** and check on the **Enable Location Services** checkbox. (You may need to click the lock in the bottom left corner and enter your sign-in password before you can make any changes.)
Maps can be used without Location Services but this would mean that Maps cannot use your current location or determine information in relation to this.

 Click on this button on the Dock or in the Launchpad

 Click on this button to view your current location

3 Double-click to zoom in on the map. Alt + double-click to zoom out. Or, swipe outwards with thumb and forefinger to zoom in, and pinch inwards to zoom out

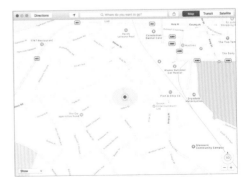

4 Or, click on these buttons to zoom in and out on a map and also view it in 3D (see next page)

Finding locations

Locations in Maps can be found for addresses, cities or landmarks. To find items in Maps:

1 Enter a term into the Search box and click on one of the results

2 The selected item is displayed and shown on a map. Pins are also dropped at this point to mark the location

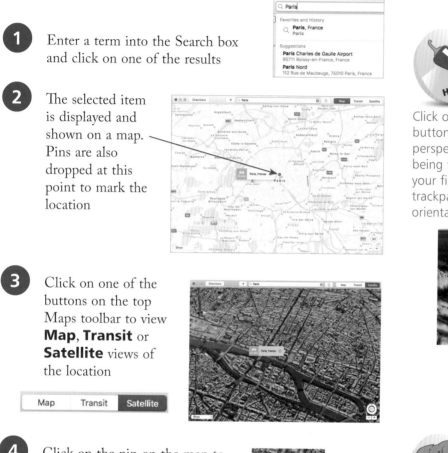

3 Click on one of the buttons on the top Maps toolbar to view **Map**, **Transit** or **Satellite** views of the location

4 Click on the pin on the map to select the location

5 Click here to view more details about the location, including options for adding it to contact information and getting directions to the location. You can also access a **Flyover Tour** of the location (if available)

Hot tip

Click on the 3D button to change the perspective of the map being viewed. Rotate your fingers on the trackpad to change the orientation of the map.

Don't forget

Flyover Tour (if available for a location) provides an animated 3D experience that travels through the most notable sights for that location.

...cont'd

Getting directions

Within Maps you can also get directions to most locations.

Don't forget

Click on this button in Step 2 to swap the locations for which you want directions.

1 Click on the **Directions** button

 Directions

2 By default, your current location is used for the **Start** field. If you want to change this, click once and enter a new location

3 Enter an **End** location or address

Don't forget

Click on the **Walk** button in Step 2 to view the directions by foot instead of car.

4 Click on one of the options for reaching your destination (**Drive**, **Walk** or **Transit**). The route is shown on the map, with the directions down the left-hand side of the window. The default mode of transport is for driving

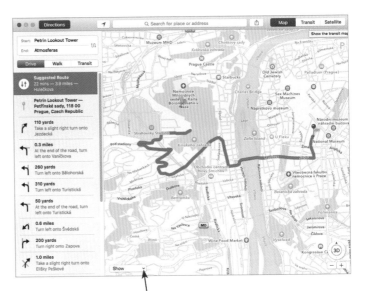

Hot tip

Click on the **Share** button to send the directions to a mobile device, such as an iPhone or an iPad, so that you can follow the directions on the go.

5 Click on the **Show** button to view the map in 3D, or for Traffic which shows any traffic disruption

Finding transit directions

In macOS Sierra there is an option for accessing transit options between two locations. To do this:

1 Enter the two locations, as shown on the previous page. Click on the **Transit** button

2 The transit options are shown in the left-hand panel

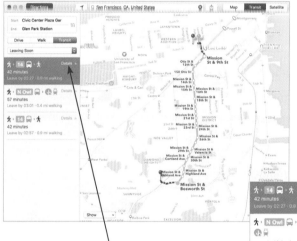

Hot tip

Click on the **Leaving Soon** box in Step 1 to specify a time for when your journey will be taking place. The transit details will be updated according to your leaving time.

3 Click on the **Details** button next to an option to view its full details. This will include any parts of the journey where you will have to walk between the transit services required for your journey

Don't forget

The Transit option is only available for a limited number of locations around the world; the majority being in the US.

Preview

Preview is a macOS app that can be used to view multiple file types, particularly image file formats. This can be useful if you just want to view documents without editing them in a dedicated app, such as an image editing app. Preview in macOS Sierra can also be used to store and view documents in iCloud.

To open Preview, click on this icon in the Applications folder in the Finder, or in the Launchpad:

Preview

Preview is also a good option for viewing PDF (Portable Document Format) documents.

 Open Preview and click on one of the options in the Finder sidebar. This includes a link to Preview in iCloud, but other locations can be used too

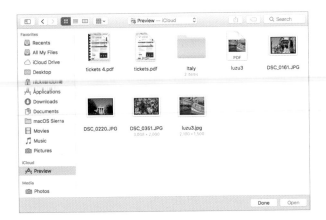

 Double-click on an item to view it at full size. This can be from any of the folders within the Finder. The item is opened in the Preview window

Printing

macOS Sierra makes the printing process as simple as possible, partly by its ability to automatically install new printers as soon as they are connected to your Mac. However, it is also possible to install printers manually. To do this:

1 Open **System Preferences** and click on the **Printers & Scanners** button

Printers & Scanners

2 Currently installed printers are displayed in the Printers list. Click here to add a new printer

$+$

3 Select an available printer

Name

Dell Laser Printer 1720dn

4 Click on the **Add** button to load the printer drivers for the selected printer

Add

5 The printer drivers are added

Setting up 'Dell Laser Printer 1720dn...'

Setting up the device...

Configure   Cancel

6 The printer is added in the **Printers & Scanners** window, under the **Printers** list, ready for use

Printers & Scanners

Q Search

Printers

Dell Laser Printer 172...
• idle

Dell Laser Printer 172...
• Offline, Last Used

Dell Laser Printer 1720dn

Open Print Queue...

Options & Supplies...

Location:

Kind: Generic PostScript Printer

Status: Idle

Share this printer on the network   Sharing Preferences...

Default printer: Last Printer Used

Default paper size: A4

Don't forget

For most printers, macOS will detect them when they are first connected and they should be ready to use, without the need to install any software or apply new settings.

Don't forget

Once a printer has been installed, documents can be printed by selecting **File** > **Print** from the Menu bar. Print settings can be set at this point and they can also be set by selecting **File** > **Page/Print Setup** from the Menu bar in most apps.

macOS Utilities

In addition to the apps in the Applications folder, there are also a number of utility apps that perform a variety of tasks within macOS. (Some of the utilities vary depending on the hardware setup of your Mac.) To access the Utilities:

The Utilities folder is also available from within the Applications folder. On some systems it may appear as "Other" in the Launchpad.

The utilities are the workhorses of macOS. They do not have the glamour of apps such as iTunes but they perform vital gathering of information and general maintenance tasks.

You may never need to use a utility like the Console, but it is worth having a look at it just to see the inner workings of a computer.

 1   Access the Launchpad to access the Utilities folder. The utilities are displayed within the Utilities folder

- **Activity Monitor**. This contains information about the system memory being used and disk activity (see page 180 for more details).

- **AirPort Utility**. This sets up the AirPort wireless networking facility that can be used to connect to the internet with a Wi-Fi connection.

- **Audio MIDI Setup**. This can be used for adding audio devices and setting their properties.

- **Bluetooth File Exchange**. This determines how files are exchanged between your computer and other Bluetooth devices (if this function is enabled).

- **Boot Camp Assistant**. This can be used to run Windows operating systems on your Mac.

- **ColorSync Utility**. This can be used to view and create color profiles on your computer. These can then be used by apps to try to match output color with monitor color.

- **Console**. This displays the behind-the-scenes messages that are being passed around the computer while its usual tasks are being performed.

- **Digital Color Meter**. This can be used to measure the exact color values of a particular color.

- **Disk Utility**. This can be used to view information about attached disks and repair errors.

- **Grab**. This is a utility which can be used to capture screen shots, which are images of the screen at a given point in time. You can grab different portions of the screen, including a timed option, and even menus. The resultant images can be saved into different file formats.

The Grab utility is useful if you are producing manuals or books and need to display examples of a screen or app.

- **Grapher**. This is a utility for creating simple or more complex scientific graphs.

- **Keychain Access**. This deals with items such as passwords when they are needed for networking. These do not have to be set but it can save time if you have to enter passwords on a lot of occasions. It also ensures that there is greater security for items protected by passwords.

- **Migration Assistant**. This helps in the transfer of files between two Mac computers. This can be used if you buy a new Mac and you need to transfer files from another one.

Other useful apps you can find in the Utilities/ Other folder are:

Stickies. This can be used to attach short notes to the screen.

- **Script Editor**. This can be used to create your own scripts with Apple's dedicated scripting app, AppleScript.

- **System Information**. This contains details of the hardware devices and software applications that are installed on your computer (see page 179 for more details).

Image Capture. This can be used to capture images or transfer and scan images.

- **Terminal**. This is used as an entry point into the world of UNIX. Within the Terminal you can view the workings of UNIX and also start to write your own apps, if you have some UNIX programming knowledge.

Ink. This can be used to add sketches and handwritten items (using a compatible graphics tablet).

- **VoiceOver Utility**. This has various options for how the VoiceOver function works within macOS. This is the digital voice that can be used to read out what is on the screen, and it is particularly useful for users who are visually impaired.

Creating PDF Documents

PDF (Portable Document Format) is a file format that preserves the formatting of an original document and it can also be viewed on a variety of computer platforms including Mac, Windows and UNIX. macOS has a built-in PDF function that can produce PDF files from many apps. To do this:

PDF files can be viewed with the Preview app.

 Open a file in an app and select **File** > **Export as PDF...**,

Export as PDF...

or use the **File** > **Save As...** option, and change the format of the document to PDF, where offered

2 Browse to a destination for the file and click **Save**

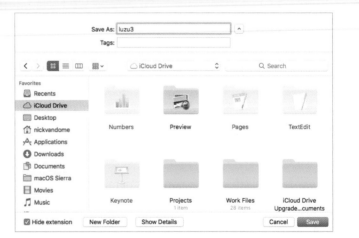

Hot tip

PDF is an excellent option if you are creating documents such as instruction booklets, magazines or manuals.

3 Locate the selected destination to view and open the newly created PDF file. You can then access options for viewing, sharing or marking up the document

7 Internet and Email

This chapter shows how to get the most out of the internet and email. It covers connecting to the internet and how to use the macOS web browser, Safari, and its email app, Mail. It also covers Messages for text messaging with a range of innovative effects.

132   Getting Connected

134   Safari

135   Safari Sidebar

136   Safari Tabbed Browsing

137   Safari Top Sites

138   Adding Bookmarks

139   Safari Reader

140   Mail

141   Using Mail

142   Messaging

144   FaceTime

Getting Connected

Connecting to the internet with a Mac is set up through the System Preferences. To do this:

Don't forget

Before you connect to the internet you must have an Internet Service Provider (ISP) who will provide you with the relevant method of connection, e.g. cable, broadband or dial-up (if being used). They will also provide you with any passwords (for connecting to a Wi-Fi router) and log in details.

1 Click on the **System Preferences** icon on the Dock

2 Click on the **Network** button

Network

3 Check that your method of connecting to the internet is active, i.e. colored green

4 Click on the **Assist me...** button to access wizards for connecting to the internet for different methods of connection

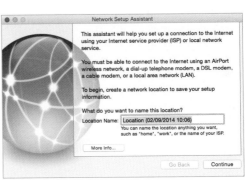

Assist Me...

5 Click on the **Assistant...** button

Assistant...

6 The **Network Setup Assistant** helps to configure your system so that you can connect to the internet

7 Enter a name for your connection

Location Name: Home Wi-Fi

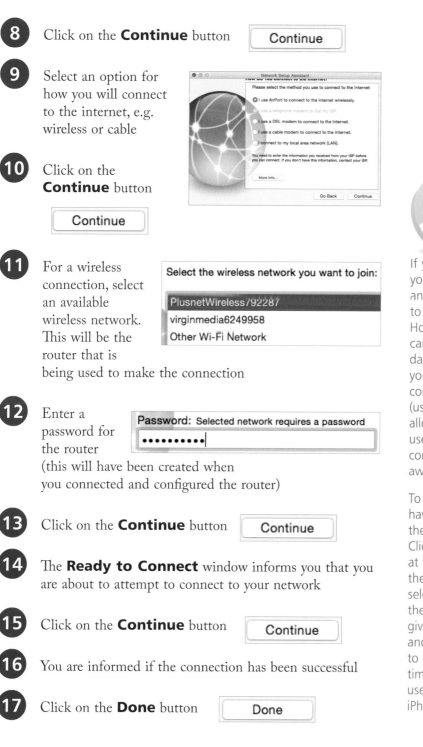

8 Click on the **Continue** button   Continue

9 Select an option for how you will connect to the internet, e.g. wireless or cable

10 Click on the **Continue** button

Continue

11 For a wireless connection, select an available wireless network. This will be the router that is being used to make the connection

Select the wireless network you want to join:

PlusnetWireless/92287
virginmedia6249958
Other Wi-Fi Network

12 Enter a password for the router

Password: Selected network requires a password
•••••••••

(this will have been created when you connected and configured the router)

13 Click on the **Continue** button   Continue

14 The **Ready to Connect** window informs you that you are about to attempt to connect to your network

15 Click on the **Continue** button   Continue

16 You are informed if the connection has been successful

17 Click on the **Done** button   Done

Hot tip

If you have an iPhone you can use your Mac and macOS Sierra to create a Personal Hotspot, so that you can use the cellular data connection from your iPhone as a Wi-Fi connection for your Mac (using your iPhone data allowance), if you cannot use your own Wi-Fi connection or you are away from home.

To do this, both devices have to be signed in to the same iCloud account. Click on the Wi-Fi icon at the right-hand side of the top Menu bar and select your iPhone from the Wi-Fi menu. This will give you online access and you can reconnect to the Hotspot the next time that you want to use it, as long as your iPhone is near your Mac.

133

Safari

Safari is a web browser that is designed specifically to be used with macOS. It is similar in most respects to other browsers, but it usually functions more quickly with macOS.

Safari overview

 Click here on the Dock to launch Safari

 All of the controls are at the top of the browser

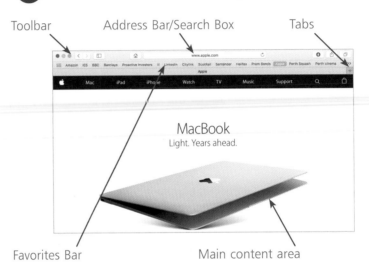

Toolbar   Address Bar/Search Box   Tabs

MacBook
Light. Years ahead.

Favorites Bar   Main content area

Address Bar/Search Box

In Safari, the Address Bar and the Search Box is combined, and can be used for searching for an item or entering a web address to go to that page:

1 Click in the Address Bar/Search Box

Q Search or enter website name

2 Select an item from the Favorites page that appears, or enter a web address or search item into the box. Options will be displayed below the Address Bar/Search Box

Safari Sidebar

A useful feature in Safari is the Safari sidebar. This is a panel in which you can view all of your Bookmarks, Reading List items and Shared Links from social media sites such as Twitter and LinkedIn.

1 Select **View** > **Show Sidebar** from the Safari Menu bar or click on this button

2 Click on the **Bookmarks** button to view all of the items that you have bookmarked (see page 138). Click on the plus symbol **+** at the bottom of the sidebar panel to add more folders for your bookmarks

3 Click on the **Reading List** button to view all of the items that you have added to your reading list so that they can be read later, even if you are offline and not connected to the internet. These can be added from the **Share** button

4 Click on the **Shared Links** button to view items that have been posted by your contacts on social media sites and any web feeds that have been added

Hot tip

Links to social networking accounts can be set up in **System Preferences** > **Internet Accounts**. Select the required account and enter the details with which you log in to it. Updates will then be available in the Shared Links panel of the sidebar.

Hot tip

To add items to the Shared Links panel, click on the button in Step 4 and click on the **Subscriptions** button at the bottom of the panel. From here, you will be able to select **Add Account** or **Add Feed** to add links from social media sites or web page feeds.

Safari Tabbed Browsing

Tabs are now a familiar feature on web browsers, so you can have multiple sites open within the same browser window:

Don't forget

Safari is a full screen app and can be expanded by clicking the double arrow in the top right corner. For more information on full screen apps, see pages 102-103.

Hot tip

Select **Safari > Preferences** from the Menu bar to specify settings for the way Safari operates.

Don't forget

If you have open tabs on other Apple devices, e.g. other Mac computers, iPads or iPhones, these will be listed at the bottom of the window in Step 5. Click on an item to open it in Safari on your Mac.

 When more than one tab is open, the tabs appear at the top of the web pages

| Apple - OS X Yosemite - Overview | In Easy Steps Smart Learning with In Easy Steps books | + |

2 Click on this button on the far right of the tabs to open a new tab

3 Click on one of the **Top Sites** (see next page) or enter a website address in the Address Bar

4 Click on this button next to the New Tab button to minimize all of the current tabs

5 Move left and right to view all of the open tabs in thumbnail view. Click on one to view it at full size

Safari Top Sites

Within Safari there is a facility to view a page showing thumbnails of the websites that you visit most frequently. This can be done from a button on the Safari Menu bar. To do this:

1 Click on this button to view the **Top Sites** window

2 The Top Sites window contains thumbnails of the websites that you have visited most frequently with Safari (this builds up as you visit more sites)

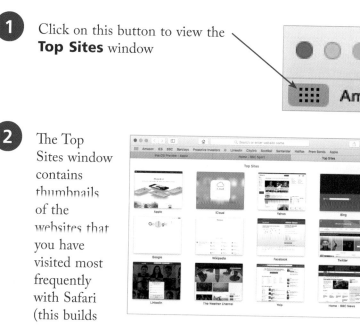

Don't forget

By default, the Top Sites window is also accessed automatically as a landing page if you open a new tab within Safari. However, this can be changed within **Safari > Preferences**. Click on the **General** tab and select an option for **New tabs open with**. This can also be done for **New windows open with**.

3 Move the cursor over a thumbnail and click on the cross to delete a thumbnail from the **Top Sites** window. Click on the pin to keep it there permanently

The Weather Channel

Hot tip

Top Sites can also be added by opening the **Sidebar** (see page 135) and dragging a bookmarked site into the Top Sites window.

4 Click on a thumbnail to go to the full site

Adding Bookmarks

Bookmarks is a feature with which you can create quick links to your favorite web pages or the ones you visit most frequently. Bookmarks can be added to a menu or the Bookmarks panel in Safari which makes them even quicker to access. Folders can also be created to store the less frequently used bookmarks. To view and create bookmarks:

Beware

Bookmarks can be added to the Favorites Bar, which can be displayed at the top of the Safari window, below the Address Bar. To add bookmarks to the Favorites Bar, select **Favorites** for **Add this page to:** in Step 4. To show (or hide) the Favorites Bar, select **View > Show Favorites Bar** (or **Hide Favorites Bar**) from the Safari Menu bar. The Favorites folder is displayed at the top of the Bookmarks panel.

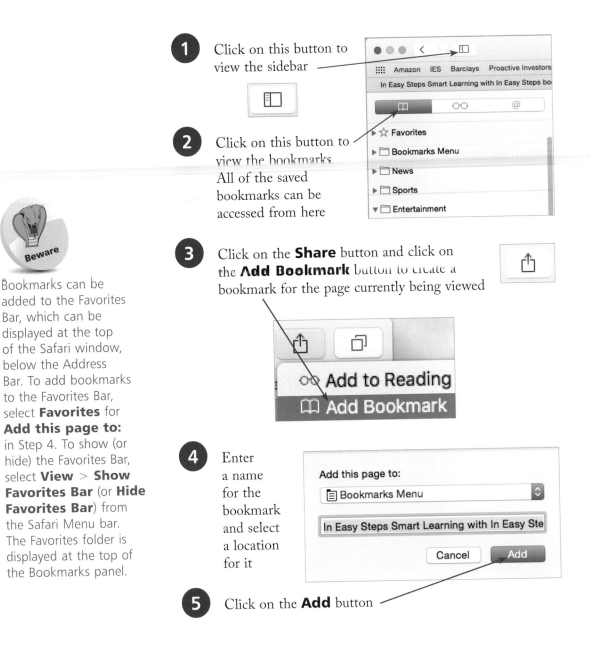

1 Click on this button to view the sidebar

2 Click on this button to view the bookmarks. All of the saved bookmarks can be accessed from here

3 Click on the **Share** button and click on the **Add Bookmark** button to create a bookmark for the page currently being viewed

Add to Reading
Add Bookmark

4 Enter a name for the bookmark and select a location for it

Add this page to:

Bookmarks Menu

In Easy Steps Smart Learning with In Easy Ste

Cancel   Add

5 Click on the **Add** button

Safari Reader

Web pages can be complex and cluttered things at times. On occasion, you may want to just read the content of one story on a web page without all of the extra material in view. In Safari this can be done with the Reader function. To do this:

 1 Select **View** > **Show Reader** from the Safari Menu bar

View   History   Bookmarks
✓ Always Show Toolbar in Full
Customize Toolbar...

Hide Favorites Bar
Hide Tab Bar
Hide Status Bar

Show Sidebar
Show Bookmarks Sidebar
Show Reading List Sidebar
Show Shared Links Sidebar

Show Reader

2 Click on the **Reader** button in the Address Bar of a web page that supports this functionality

≡ ⊕   Show Reader View

3 The button turns black once the Reader is activated

4 The content is displayed in a text format, with a minimum of formatting from the original page

Thinkstock

Rapid diagnostic tests are urgently needed to help doctors know which patients need antibiotics, a report says.

The Review on Antimicrobial Resistance calls for tests to indentify viral and bacterial infections.

Only bacterial infections respond to antibiotics.

The review team said such tests could end "just in case" prescribing which sees a huge proportion of antibiotics used needlessly.

The review was set up last year by the Prime Minister David Cameron, who warned the world risked being plunged back into the Dark Ages of medicine by the overuse of antibiotics.

5 Click on the **Share** button on the Safari toolbar if you want to save a page to read later

⬆   ❐

∞ Add to Reading List

6 Click on this button to add the page to your Reading List

Beware

Not all web pages support the Reader functionality in Safari.

Hot tip

Pages that are saved to your Reading List with the button in Step 6 can be read when you are offline, so you do not need to be connected to the internet.

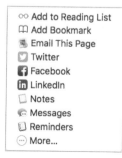
Don't forget

Other options can also be accessed from the **Share** button: ⬆

∞ Add to Reading List
⬚ Add Bookmark
🖼 Email This Page
🐦 Twitter
📘 Facebook
in LinkedIn
🗒 Notes
💬 Messages
🔖 Reminders
⋯ More...

Mail

Email is an essential element for most computer users and Macs come with their own email app called Mail. This covers all of the email functionality that most people could need.

When first using Mail you have to set up your email account. This can be done with most email accounts and also a wide range of web mail accounts, including iCloud. To add email accounts:

Don't forget

Mail is a full screen app. For more information on full screen apps, see pages 102-103.

1 Click on this icon on the Dock

2 Check on the button next to the type of account that you want to add to the Mail app, e.g. if you have an iCloud account, select iCloud to add this

Choose a Mail account provider...

○ iCloud
○ 🅴Exchange
○ Google
○ YAHOO!
○ Aol.
○ Other Mail Account...

? Cancel Continue

Don't forget

You can set up more than one account in the Mail app and you can download messages from all of the accounts that you set up. To set up an account from the Mail app, select **Mail** > **Account** from the Menu bar.

3 Enter details of the account and click on the **Sign In** button

Sign in to use your Apple ID.
If you have an Apple ID, sign in with it here. If you have used the iTunes Store or iCloud, for example, you have an Apple ID. If you don't have an Apple ID, click Create Apple ID.

Apple ID | Password | Forgot?
nickvandome@mac.com | •••••••

Create Apple ID | Cancel | Sign In

4 Check the **Mail** option for iCloud to sync your iCloud email across any other Apple devices and also your online account at **www.icloud.com**

☁ iCloud

Account: nickvandome@mac.com
Use with:
☑ iCloud Drive
☐ Photos
☑ Mail
☑ Contacts
☑ Calendars
☑ Reminders

Cancel | Go Back | Add Account

Using Mail

Mail enables you to send and receive emails and also format them to your own style. This can be simply formatting text, or attaching images or documents. To use Mail:

1 Click on the **Get Mail** button to download available email messages

2 Click on the **New Message** button to create a new email

3 Click on the **Format** button to access options for formatting the text in the email

4 Click on these buttons to **Reply** to, **Reply** (to) **All** or **Forward** an email you have received

5 Select or open an email and click on the **Trash** button to delete it

6 Click on the **Junk** button to mark an email as junk or spam. This trains Mail to identify junk mail. After a period of time, these types of messages will automatically be moved straight into the Junk mailbox

7 Click on the **Attach** button to browse your folders to include a file in your email. This can be items such as photos, Word documents or PDF files

8 Use these buttons in the New Message window to select fonts and font size, color, bold, italic, underlining, strikethrough and alignment options

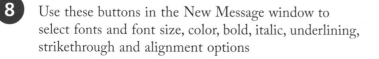

To show the descriptive text underneath an icon in Mail, Ctrl + click next to an icon and select **Icon & Text** from the menu.

When entering the name of a recipient for a message, Mail will display details of matching names from the Contacts app. For instance, if you type "DA", all of the entries in your Contacts beginning with this will be displayed and you then can select the required one.

If you forward an email with an attachment, then the attachment is included. If you reply to an email, the attachment will not be included.

Messaging

The Messages app enables you to send text messages (iMessages) to other macOS Sierra users or those with an iPhone, iPad or iPod Touch using iOS. It can also be used to send photos, videos and make FaceTime calls. To use Messages:

iMessages are specific to Apple and sent over Wi-Fi. SMS (Short Message Service) messages are usually sent between cellular devices, such as smartphones, that are contracted to a compatible mobile services provider.

1 Click on this icon on the Dock

2 You need an Apple ID to use Messages and you will need to enter these details when you first access it. If you do not have an Apple ID you will be able to create one at this point

3 Click on this button to start a new conversation

Don't forget

Messages in macOS Sierra supports emojis that can be included by clicking on the emoji icon at the right-hand side of the text box. The emojis can be selected from a large menu, split into categories including animals and nature, food, activity and travel.

4 Click on this button and select a contact (these will be from your Contacts app). To send an iMessage, the recipient must have an Apple ID

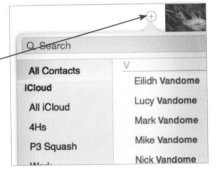

5 The person with whom you are having a conversation is displayed in the left-hand panel

6 The conversation continues down the right-hand panel. Click here to write a message and press **Return** to send

Adding photos and videos

Photos and videos can be added to messages:

1 Select the photo or video in the Finder, next to the Messages app

2 Drag the photo or video into the text box to include it in the message

Text forwarding

If you have an iPhone you can receive and send SMS text messages through your Mac with macOS Sierra. To use your Mac to send and receive SMS messages:

1 On your Mac, from the Messages menu click on **Messages > Preferences > Accounts**. Click on the **iMessages** account button in the left-hand panel and check **On** your own phone number and email address

2 On your iPhone, select **Settings > Messages > Send & Receive** and add your email address

3 Then, also on your iPhone, select **Settings > Messages > Text Message Forwarding** and turn **On** text forwarding for the required device(s)

4 An activation code appears on your Mac; enter this on your iPhone to enable text forwarding

To delete a conversation, hover over it in the left-hand panel and click on this cross.

Audio messages can also be included in an iMessage. Click on this icon to the right of the text box and record your message.

Messages in macOS Sierra also supports Tapback, whereby you can add an icon to a message as a quick reply. To do this, click and hold on a message text and click on an icon.

FaceTime

FaceTime is an app that can be used to make video and audio calls to other Macs, iPhones, iPads and iPod Touches. To use FaceTime on your Mac you must have an in-built FaceTime camera or use a compatible external one. To use FaceTime:

Don't forget

If you receive a video call, you are alerted to this even if FaceTime is not open or running.

1 Click on this icon on the Dock

Hot tip

In a similar way to text forwarding, macOS Sierra on a Mac can also be used for Phone Call Forwarding from your iPhone. Both devices need to have Wi-Fi turned on and be signed into the same iCloud account. On your Mac, select **FaceTime > Preferences** from the FaceTime menu and check **On**, **Calls From iPhone** (from the Settings tab). On your iPhone, access **Settings > Phone** and drag the **Allow Calls on Other Devices** to **On** and select the required devices under the **Allow Calls On** section. When you receive a call, it shows up as a notification on your Mac via FaceTime and you can Accept or Decline it.

2 You need an Apple ID to use FaceTime. Enter your details and click on the **Sign in** button

3 Once you have logged in you can make video calls by selecting people from your address book, providing they have an Apple ID and a device that supports FaceTime. Either start typing a contact's name, email address or phone number into the Search box, or click on this button to access your Contacts address book

(8) Digital Lifestyle

Leisure time, and how we use it, is an important consideration for everyone. This chapter details some of the options with macOS Sierra, including the Photos app and iTunes for music.

146 Using the Photos App

147 Viewing Photos

149 Editing Photos

150 Photo Memories

152 Starting with iTunes

153 Buying Music with iTunes

154 Using Apple Music

155 Reading with iBooks

Using the Photos App

For a number of years the photo management and editing tool for OS X was iPhoto. However, in Spring 2015 the Photos app was introduced. iPhoto can still be used, but the Photos app is designed to mirror the one used on iOS 9 devices (and later) and integrate more with iCloud, so that you can store all of your photos in the iCloud and then view and manage them on all of your Apple devices.

If you are using the Photos app, you can specify how it operates with iCloud in the iCloud System Preferences:

1 Click on the **System Preferences** button

2 Click on the **iCloud** button in the System Preferences window

3 Check **On** the **Photos** checkbox

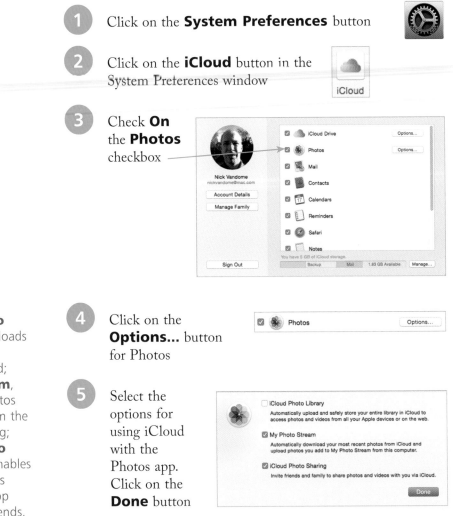

Don't forget

The iCloud options for the Photos app are: **iCloud Photo Library**, which uploads your entire photo library to the iCloud; **My Photo Stream**, which uploads photos that are added from the device you are using; and **iCloud Photo Sharing**, which enables you to share photos from the Photos app with family and friends.

4 Click on the **Options...** button for Photos

5 Select the options for using iCloud with the Photos app. Click on the **Done** button

Viewing Photos

The Photos app can be used to view photos according to Years, Collections, Moments or at full size. This enables you to view your photos according to dates and times at which they were taken.

1. Open the Photos app, and click on these buttons at the top of the window to move between Years, Collections and Moments

2. If you are viewing Collections, click on the left-hand button in Step 1 to move to **Years** view

3. Click and hold on a thumbnail in Years view to enlarge it

4. Click on a photo within the Years section to view the **Collections**. This displays groups of photos (Moments) taken at the same location or date range

When you first open the Photos app you can select current photo libraries to import. This will ensure that all of the photos you want are available in the Photos app when you start.

Photos can be imported into the Photos app by selecting **File** > **Import** from the Menu bar and navigating to the required location within the Finder. This can be used to import photos from your Mac or an external device connected with a USB cable, such as a digital camera, a card reader or a flashdrive.

...cont'd

5 Click on a photo within the Collections section to view specific **Moments**. This displays photos taken at the same time in the same location

Don't forget

Drag this slider at the top of the window to change the magnification of the photo (or photos) being displayed in Moments, or at full size view.

6 Double-click on a photo in the Collections or Moments section to view it at full size

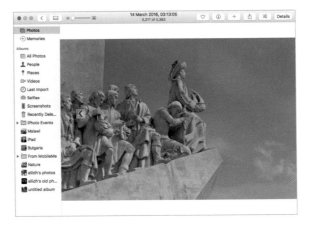

7 For a photo displayed at full size, use these buttons from left to right to: add it as a favorite; view information about it; add the photo to a new or existing album, order prints, a photo book, calendar or card, or add it to a slideshow; share the photo; edit it (see next page); or view its details

Editing Photos

The Photos app has a range of editing options that can be used to enhance your photos. To do this:

1 Open a photo at full size

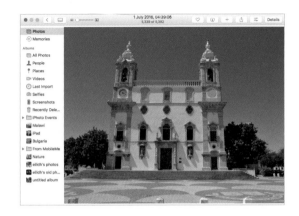

2 Click on this button

3 The editing options are displayed at the right-hand side of the screen. Click on one to access its specific settings

4 Some editing options, such as **Filters**, have a one-click option for applying the effect. Others, such as **Adjust**, have a range of panels which can be used to make specific editing changes, such as to the light or color of a photo. Some of these panels also have an **Auto** option

Don't forget

Click on the **Done** button at the top of the Photos app window to apply any editing changes that have been made. Click on the **Revert to Original** to discard the changes (this can also be done when you return to a photo that has been edited).

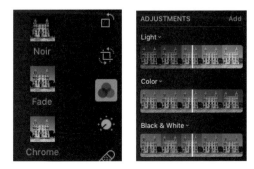

Photo Memories

Selecting your best photos is sometimes a challenge, but the Photos app now does this automatically, through the use of the Memories function. This displays photos based on locations, people and times and a slideshow is also created from the photos. To use the Memories option:

 Click on the **Memories** button in the left-hand sidebar of the Photos app

 Click on the **Get Started** button to enable the Photos app to scan your photos to create the necessary collections of memories

Memories

Photos scans your library to create a collection of memories based on location, time, and the people in your pictures.

New Memories appear daily in the Memories tab.

Get Started

Hot tip

Click on the **People** or **Places** button in the left-hand sidebar to view collections of photos of specific people (based on the results of the Photos app scanning all of the available photos and identifying people within them); or locations where photos have been taken.

👤 People
📍 Places

The different collections of memories are displayed on the Memories homepage. Click on one to view its photos

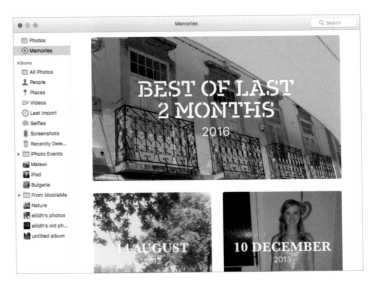

4 Scroll through a memory collection to view the photos

Don't forget

The slideshow at the top of the Memories homepage starts playing as soon as the page is accessed.

5 The top panel of each memory collection displays the photos as an automated slideshow

Don't forget

Scroll to the bottom of the Memories homepage to view **Related** items that can also be viewed as memories. Memories can also be added as favorites, which creates a **Favorite Memories** button in the left-hand sidebar.

6 Scroll to the bottom of a memory collection to view the location of the photos shown on a map

Hot tip

Click on the Edit button in a memory collection to customize the slideshow.

Starting with iTunes

Music is one of the areas that has revived Apple's fortunes in recent years, primarily through the music player iTunes, and also the iTunes music store, where music can be bought online. iTunes is a versatile app but its basic function is to play a music CD. To do this:

Don't forget

iMovie and GarageBand are two other Apple apps for creating home movies and music respectively, which come pre-installed on qualifying new Macs. There is also a range of apps for creating DVDs in the App Store.

Beware

Never import music and use it for commercial purposes as this would be a breach of copyright.

Hot tip

Notifications can be set to display each iTunes item as it is being played. To do this, ensure **iTunes** is selected in **Notifications** within **System Preferences**. Access the Notifications (see page 120) and the currently playing item will be displayed.

1   Click on this button on the Dock and insert the CD in the CD/DVD drive (internal if provided, or an external CD/DVD drive

2   By default, iTunes will open and display this window. Click **No** if you just want to play the CD

Would you like to import the CD "Mozart: Le Nozze Di Figaro (Highlights)" into your iTunes library?
☐ Do not ask me again
No   Yes

3   Click on this button to access the CD and double-click on a track to play it, or

Mozart: Le Nozze Di Figaro (Highlights)
23 songs • 1 hour, 12 minutes

4   Click on this button to play a track or a whole CD

5   Click on the **Import CD** button if you want to copy the music from the CD onto your hard drive

Buying Music with iTunes

As well as copying music from CDs into iTunes, it is also possible to download a vast selection of music from the iTunes Store online. To do this:

1 Click on the **Store** button to access the online store

2 Navigate around the iTunes Store using the panels and sections within the Store homepage

3 To find a specific item, enter the details in the **Search** box at the top right-hand corner of the iTunes window

4 Details of the item are displayed within the Store. Click on the price button to buy (or the Get button if the item is free) and download it. This will appear in the **Library** section of your iTunes app

Beware

Never use illegal music download sites. Apart from the legal factor, they are much more likely to contain viruses and spyware.

Don't forget

To buy music from the iTunes Store you must have an Apple ID and a linked credit or debit card for purchases.

Don't forget

Click on the **All Genres** drop-down list underneath the **Music** heading in the iTunes window to select different genres to view.

Using Apple Music

Apple Music is a service that makes the entire Apple iTunes library of music available to users. It is a subscription service, and music can be streamed over the internet or downloaded so you can listen to it when you are offline. To start with Apple Music:

Don't forget

Numerous radio stations can also be listened to through Apple Music, including Beats 1.

Hot tip

Click on the **Connect** button on the top toolbar to select artists to follow so that you get the latest music information and updates about them.

154

Hot tip

To end your Apple Music subscription at any point, open **iTunes** and select **Account > View My Account...** from the Menu bar. Sign in with your Apple ID and in the **Account Information** window, under **Settings** click on the **Subscriptions > Manage** button. Click on the **Edit** button and drag the **Automatic Renewal** button to **Off**. You can then renew your Apple Music membership, if required, by selecting one of the **Options**.

1 Click on the **iTunes** icon

2 Click on the **For You** button on the top toolbar

For You

3 Click on the **Choose Your Plan** button to select a monthly subscription option (this option is available after the initial three-month free trial has been used)

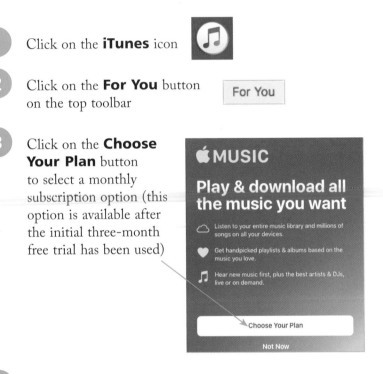

4 Click on the **Recommendations** button to view suggested playlists or specific tracks. These can all be played directly using streaming over Wi-Fi, or downloaded to be played offline

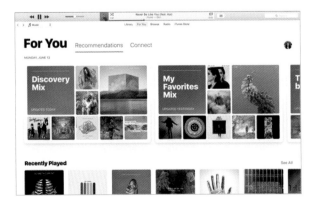

Reading with iBooks

iBooks is an eBook reading app that has been available with Apple's mobile devices, including the iPhone and the iPad, for a number of years. macOS Sierra also offers this technology for desktop and laptop Macs. To use iBooks:

1 Click on this icon on the Dock or within the Launchpad

Don't forget

iBooks consists of your own library for storing and reading eBooks, and also access to the online **iBooks Store** for buying and downloading new books. Items that you have downloaded with iBooks on other devices will also be available in your iBooks Library on your Mac.

2 Click on the **Get Started** button

3 Click on the **Sign In** button to sign in with your Apple ID and access the iBooks Store

4 If you are signed in with your Apple ID, click on the **iBooks Store** button

iBooks Store

5 The iBooks Store contains a wide range of books that can be previewed and downloaded

Hot tip

Use these buttons on the top toolbar of the iBooks Store to view books by **Featured**, **Top Charts**, **Categories** and **Top Authors**.

6 Click on a title to preview details about it

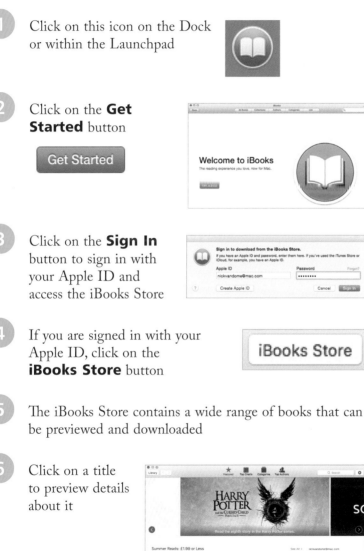

...cont'd

Don't forget

From the iBooks Store, click on the **Library** button in the top left-hand corner to go back to your own Library.

Don't forget

Use these buttons on the top toolbar of a book to, from left to right, go back to your Library, view the table of contents or view any notes you have added.

To add a note, select text and then click Add Note.

Don't forget

Use these buttons on the top toolbar to, from left to right, change the text size, search for text and add a bookmark to a page.

7 Click on the price button to download the book (if it is free, this button will display **Get**). You will be asked to enter your Apple ID password to confirm the purchase

8 The title will be downloaded into your iBooks Library. When it has finished downloading, click on the **Read** button. Or, from your Library, double-click on the cover to open the book and start reading

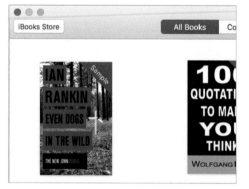

9 Click or tap on the right-hand or left-hand edges to turn a page. Move the cursor over the top of the page to access the top toolbar. The bottom toolbar displays the page numbers and location

9 Sharing macOS

This chapter looks at how to set up and manage different user accounts on your Mac.

158 Adding Users

160 Deleting Users

161 Fast User Switching

162 Parental Controls

Adding Users

macOS enables multiple users to access individual accounts on the same computer. If there are multiple users, i.e. two or more for a single machine, each person can log in individually and access their own files and folders. This means that each person can log in to their own settings and preferences. All user accounts can be password protected, to ensure that each user's environment is secure. To set up multiple user accounts:

Don't forget

Every computer with multiple users has at least one main user, also known as the administrator. This means that they have greater control over the number of items that they can edit and alter. If there is only one user on a computer, they automatically take on the role of the administrator. Administrators have a particularly important role to play when computers are networked together. Each computer can potentially have several administrators.

1   Click on the **System Preferences** icon on the Dock

2   Click on the **Users & Groups** icon

3   The information about the current user account is displayed. This is your own account and the information is based on details you provided when you first set up your Mac

Don't forget

Each user can select their own icon or photo of themselves.

4   Click on this icon to enter your password to unlock the settings so that new accounts can be added

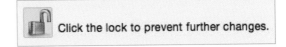

5 Click on the **+** button to add a new account

6 Enter the details for the new account holder

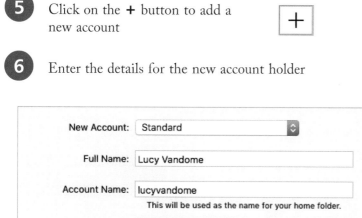

New Account: Standard

Full Name: Lucy Vandome

Account Name: lucyvandome
This will be used as the name for your home folder.

Password: ••••••••

Verify: ••••••••

Password hint: Color
(Recommended)

Cancel   Create User

7 Click on the **Create User** button

Create User

8 The new account is added to the list in the Users & Groups window, under **Other Users**

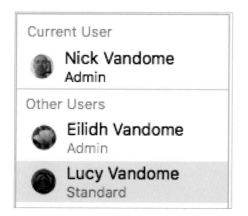

Current User
Nick Vandome
Admin

Other Users
Eilidh Vandome
Admin

Lucy Vandome
Standard

At Step 6, choose the type of account from the drop-down list. An **Administrator** account is one which allows the user to make system changes, and add or delete other users; A **Standard** account allows the user to use the functionality of the Mac, but not change system settings; **Manage with Parental Controls** is an account that can have restrictions added to it; and **Sharing Only** is an account that allows guests to log in temporarily, without a password – when they log out, all files and information will be deleted from the guest account.

By default, you are the Administrator of your own Mac. This means that you can administer other user accounts.

Deleting Users

Once a user has been added, their name appears on the list in the Users & Groups dialog box (see Step 3 on page 158). It is then possible to edit the details of the particular user or delete them altogether. To do this:

 Within **Users & Groups**, unlock the settings as shown in Step 4 on page 158, then select a user from the list

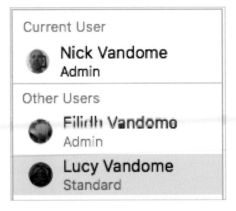

Current User

Nick Vandome
Admin

Other Users

Filidh Vandome
Admin

Lucy Vandome
Standard

 Click here to remove the selected person's user account

——

3 A warning box appears to check if you really do want to delete the selected user. If you do, select the required option and click on the **Delete User** button

Are you sure you want to delete the user account "Lucy Vandome"?

To delete this user account, select what you want to do with the home folder for this account, and then click "Delete User".

○ Save the home folder in a disk image
The disk image is saved in the Deleted Users folder (in the Users folder).

○ Don't change the home folder
The home folder remains in the Users folder.

○ Delete the home folder
☐ Erase home folder securely

Cancel   Delete User

Fast User Switching

If there are multiple users on your macOS system, it is useful to be able to switch between them as quickly as possible. When this is done, the first user's session is retained so that they can return to it if required. To switch between users:

Unlock the settings before you start (see Step 4 on page 158).

1. In the Users & Groups window, click on the **Login Options** button

2. Check **On** the **Show fast user switching menu as** box, then close the window

3. At the top right of the screen, click on the current user's name

When you switch between users, the first user remains logged in and their current session remains intact.

4. Click on the name of another user

Users can sign in from the Lock screen with a password by clicking on their own icon/name on the screen and entering the relevant details. If Fast User Switching is not used, each user has to log out before the next one can sign in.

5. Enter the relevant password (if required)

6. Click on this button to log in

Parental Controls

If children are using the computer, parents may want to restrict access to certain types of information that can be viewed, using Parental Controls. To do this:

Don't forget

Unlock the settings before you start (see Step 4 on page 158).

Hot tip

To check which sites have been viewed on a web browser, check the History menu, which is located on the main Menu bar in the Safari app.

1 Access **Users & Groups** and click on a user name. Check **On** the **Enable parental controls** box, click the Enable button, then click on the **Open Parental Controls...** button

☑ Enable parental controls   Open Parental Controls...

2 Click on the **Apps** tab   Apps

 3 Check **On** this box if you want to limit the types of app that a user can access

Ⓐ ☑ **Limit Applications on this Mac**
Allow the user to open only the specified applications on this Mac. An administrator password is required to open other applications.

Allowed Apps: Q Search

▼ ☑ Other Apps
   ☑ 🅰 AAM Updates Notifier
   ☑ 🅱 Adobe Bridge CS4
   ☑ 📰 Adobe Elements 9 Organizer
   ☑ ℹ Adobe\Help.app

4 Under **Allowed Apps**, check **Off** the boxes next to the apps that you do not want used

5 Check On or Off the items below, allowing the use of the camera and also limiting emails to allowed contacts (click on the **Manage...** button to specify allowed contacts)

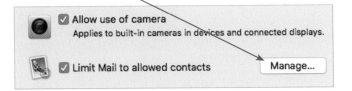

📷 ☑ Allow use of camera
Applies to built-in cameras in devices and connected displays.

🪪 ☑ Limit Mail to allowed contacts   Manage...

Web controls

 1 Click on the **Web** tab and choose one of the Browser Restrictions options:

- Check **On** this button to try to prevent access to websites with adult content. Click **Customize...** to allow or deny access to specific websites

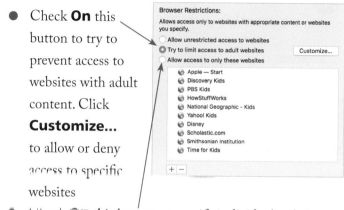

- Check **On** this button to specify individual websites that are suitable to be viewed

Stores controls

 1 Click on the **Stores** tab

2 Check **On** the items under **Disable** that you do not want available, and apply the necessary settings under **Restrict** in terms of types of content that is permissible

> Disable: ☑ iTunes Store
> ☐ iTunes U
> ☐ iBooks Store
>
> Restrict: ☑ Music with explicit content
> ☐ Movies to: 12 ⌄
> ☐ TV shows to: CAUTION ⌄
> ☑ Apps to: 12+ ⌄
> ☑ Books with explicit sexual content

Hot tip

If you are setting web controls for a child, or grandchild, discuss this with them so they understand what you are doing and why. This could also be a good time to discuss some of the issues of online security, such as never replying to any type of message or contact from people you do not know.

...cont'd

Time controls

 Click on the **Time** tab

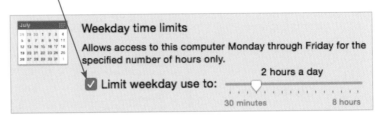 Check **On** this box to limit the amount of time the user can use the Mac during weekdays

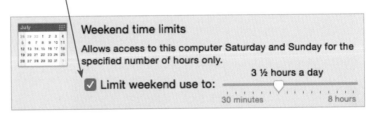

Hot tip

Time limits and other parental controls have to be set for each individual user to whom you want them to apply.

3 Check **On** this box to limit the amount of time the user can use the Mac during weekends

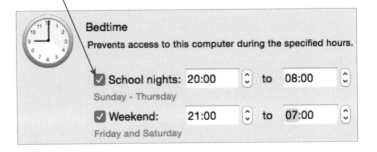

4 Check **On** these boxes to determine the times at which the user cannot access their account

10 Networking

This chapter looks at networking and how to share files over a network.

166 Networking Overview

168 Network Settings

169 File Sharing

170 Connecting to a Network

Networking Overview

Before you start sharing files directly between computers, you have to connect them together. This is known as networking and can be done with two computers in the same room, or with thousands of computers in a major corporation. If you are setting up your own small network it will be known in the computing world as a Local Area Network (LAN). When setting up a network there are various pieces of hardware that are initially required to join all of the network items together. Once this has been done, software settings can be applied for the networked items. Some of the items of hardware that may be required include:

- **A network card**. This is known as a Network Interface Card (NIC), and all recent Macs have them built in.

- **A wireless router**. This is for a wireless network, which is increasingly the most common way to create a network via Wi Fi. The router is connected to a telephone line and the computer then communicates with it wirelessly.

- **An Ethernet port and Ethernet cable**. This enables you to make the physical connection between devices. Ethernet cables come in a variety of forms, but the one you should be looking for is the Cat6 type as this allows for the fastest transfer of data. If you are creating a wireless network then you will not require these.

- **A hub**. This is a piece of hardware with multiple Ethernet ports that enables you to connect all of your devices together and lets them communicate with each other. However, conflicts can occur with hubs if two devices try to send data through one at the same time.

- **A switch**. This is similar in operation to a hub but it is more sophisticated in its method of data transfer, thus allowing all of the machines on the network to communicate simultaneously, unlike a hub.

Once you have worked out all of the devices that you want to include on your network, you can arrange them accordingly. Try to keep the switches and hub within relative proximity of a power supply and, if you are using cables, make sure they are laid out safely.

Don't forget

Connecting to the internet is also another form of network connection.

Hot tip

If you have two Macs to be networked and they are in close proximity, this can be achieved with an Ethernet crossover cable. If you have more than two computers, this is where an Ethernet hub is required. In either case, there is no need to connect to the internet to achieve the network.

Ethernet network

The cheapest and easiest way to network computers is to create an Ethernet network. This involves buying an Ethernet hub or switch, which enables you to connect several devices to a central point, i.e. the hub or switch. All Apple computers and most modern printers have an Ethernet connection, so it is possible to connect various devices, not just computers. Once all of the devices have been connected by Ethernet cables, you can then start applying network settings.

AirPort network

Another option for creating a network is using Apple's own wireless system, AirPort. This creates a wireless network and there are two main options used by Apple computers: AirPort Express, using the IEEE 802.11n standard, which is more commonly known as Wi-Fi, and the newer AirPort Extreme, using the next generation IEEE 802.11ac standard which is up to five times faster than the 802.11n standard. Thankfully, AirPort Express and Extreme are also compatible with devices based on the older IEEE standards, 802.11b/g/n, so one machine loaded with AirPort Extreme can still communicate wirelessly with the older AirPort version.

One of the main issues with a wireless network is security, since it is possible for someone with a wireless-enabled machine to access your wireless network if they are within range. However, in the majority of cases the chances of this happening are fairly slim, although it is an issue about which you should be aware.

The basic components of a wireless network between Macs are an AirPort card (either AirPort Express or AirPort Extreme) installed in all of the required machines, and an AirPort base station that can be located anywhere within 150 meters of the AirPort enabled computers. Once the hardware is in place, wireless-enabled devices can be configured using the AirPort Utility setup assistant found in the Utilities/Other folder. After AirPort has been set up, the wireless network can be connected. All of the wireless-enabled devices should then be able to communicate with each other, without the use of a multitude of cables.

Wireless network

A wireless network can also be created with a standard wireless router, rather than using the AirPort option.

Another method for connecting items wirelessly is Bluetooth. This covers much shorter distances than AirPort, and is usually used for items such as printers and smartphones. Bluetooth devices can be connected using the Bluetooth File Exchange utility: select the required files you want to exchange via Bluetooth and then select the required device.

AirPort Time Capsule is a method of backing up, using Wi-Fi instead of a cable connection. It offers up to 3TB of storage and is designed to work with Time Machine (see pages 174-177).

Network Settings

Once you have connected the hardware needed for a network, you can start applying the network settings that are required for connecting to the internet, for online access.

1 In **System Preferences**, click on the **Network** button

Network

2 For a wireless connection, click on the **Turn Wi-Fi On** button

Turn Wi-Fi On

3 Details of wireless settings are displayed

Hot tip

An Ethernet cable can be used to connect to a router instead of using a Wi-Fi connection, and it can also be used to connect two computers.

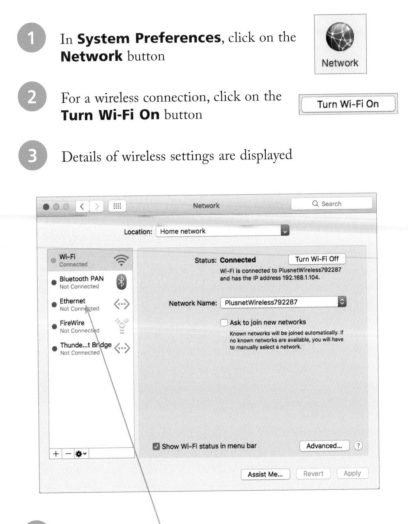

4 For a cable connection, connect an Ethernet cable and click on the **Ethernet** button

5 Click on the **Advanced...** button to see the full settings for each option

Advanced...

File Sharing

One of the main reasons for creating a network of two or more computers is to share files between them. On networked Macs, this involves setting them up so that they can share files, and then accessing these files.

Setting up file sharing

To set up file sharing on a networked Mac:

 Click on the **System Preferences** button on the Dock

 Click on the **Sharing** icon

Sharing

 Check **On** the boxes next to the items you want to share (the most common items to share are files and printers)

On	Service
☐	DVD or CD Sharing
☐	Screen Sharing
☑	File Sharing
☑	Printer Sharing
☐	Remote Login
☐	Remote Management
☐	Remote Apple Events
☐	Internet Sharing
☑	Bluetooth Sharing

Hot tip

For macOS Sierra users, files can also be shared with the AirDrop option. This can be used with two Macs and compatible iPhones and iPads that have this facility. Files can be shared simply by dragging them onto the icon of the other user that appears in the AirDrop window. To access AirDrop, click on this button in the Finder.

Connecting to a Network

Connecting as a registered user

To connect as a registered user (usually as yourself when you want to access items on another one of your own computers):

Don't forget

You can disconnect from a networked computer by ejecting it in the Finder in the same way as you would for a removable drive, such as a DVD or flashdrive (see page 53).

1 Other connected computers on the network will show up in the Shared section in the Finder. Click on a networked computer

Shared
Mac mini

2 Click on the **Connect As...** button

Connect As...

3 Check on the **Registered User** button and enter your user name and password

Enter your name and password for the server "Mac mini"

Connect As: ○ Guest
⦿ Registered User
○ Using an Apple ID

Name: nickvandome

Password: ••••••••

☐ Remember this password in my keychain

Cancel   Connect

4 Click on the **Connect** button

5 The public folders and home folder of the networked computer are available to the registered user. Double-click on an item to view its contents

Connected as: nickvandome

Name

▦ Eilidh Vandome's Public Folder
▦ Lucy Vandome's Public Folder
▦ Macintosh HD
▦ Nick Vandome's Public Folder
▦ nickvandome

Guest users

Guest users on a network are users other than yourself or other registered users, to whom you want to limit access to your files and folders. Guests only have access to a folder called the Drop Box in your own Public folder. To share files with Guest users you have to first copy them into the Drop Box. To do this:

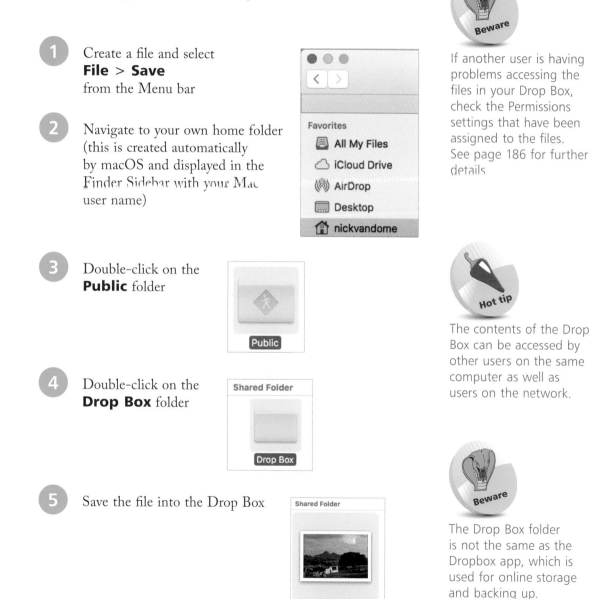

1   Create a file and select
    File > Save
    from the Menu bar

2   Navigate to your own home folder (this is created automatically by macOS and displayed in the Finder Sidebar with your Mac user name)

Favorites

All My Files
iCloud Drive
AirDrop
Desktop
nickvandome

3   Double-click on the **Public** folder

Public

4   Double-click on the **Drop Box** folder

Shared Folder

Drop Box

5   Save the file into the Drop Box

Shared Folder

malawi4.jpg

Beware

If another user is having problems accessing the files in your Drop Box, check the Permissions settings that have been assigned to the files. See page 186 for further details

Hot tip

The contents of the Drop Box can be accessed by other users on the same computer as well as users on the network.

Beware

The Drop Box folder is not the same as the Dropbox app, which is used for online storage and backing up.

...cont'd

Accessing a Drop Box

To access files in a Drop Box:

Double-click on a networked computer in the Finder

Beware

It is better to copy files into the Drop Box rather than moving them completely from their primary location.

Click on the **Connect As...** button in the Finder window

Connect As...

Check on the **Guest** button

Connect As: ● Guest
             ○ Registered User
             ○ Using an Apple ID

             Cancel   Connect

Click on the **Connect** button

Double-click on a user's **Public Folder**

Hot tip

Set Permissions for how the Drop Box operates by selecting it in the Finder and Ctrl + clicking on it. Select **Get Info** from the menu and apply the required settings under the **Sharing & Permissions** heading.

Double-click on the **Drop Box** folder to access the files within it

Nick Vandome's Public Folder

Drop Box

172

11 Maintaining macOS

Despite its stability, macOS still benefits from a robust maintenance regime. This chapter looks at ways to keep macOS in top shape, ensure downloaded apps are as secure as possible and some general troubleshooting.

174 Time Machine

178 Disk Utility

179 System Information

180 Activity Monitor

181 Updating Software

182 Gatekeeper

183 Privacy

184 Problems with Apps

185 General Troubleshooting

Time Machine

Time Machine is a feature of macOS that gives you great peace of mind. In conjunction with an external hard drive, it creates a backup of your whole system, including folders, files, apps and even the macOS operating system itself.

Once it has been set up, Time Machine takes a backup every hour and you can then go into Time Machine to restore any files that have been deleted or become corrupt since the last backup.

Setting up Time Machine

To use Time Machine, it first has to be set up. This involves attaching a hard drive to your Mac via cable or wirelessly, depending on the type of hard drive you have. To set up Time Machine:

Beware

Make sure that you have an external hard drive that is larger than the contents of your Mac, otherwise Time Machine will not be able to back it all up.

Don't forget

The hard drive must be connected in order to use Time Machine. Or, you could use AirPort Time Capsule, which is a method of backing up using Wi-Fi instead of a cable connection. It offers up to 3TB of storage and is designed to work with Time Machine.

1. Click on the **Time Machine** icon on the Dock or access it in System Preferences

2. You will be prompted to set up Time Machine

> **Your Time Machine backup disk can't be found.**
>
> Cancel   Set Up Time Machine

3. Click on the **Set Up Time Machine** button   Set Up Time Machine

4. In the Time Machine window, click on the **Select Disk...** button

Select Disk...

5 Connect an external hard drive and select it from the **Available Disks** list

6 Click on the **Use Disk** button

Use Disk

7 In the Time Machine window, check **On** the **Back Up Automatically** option

Time Machine

☑ Back Up Automatically

8 The backup will begin. The initial backup copies your whole system and can take several hours. Subsequent hourly backups only look at items that have been changed since the previous backup

9 The record of backups and the schedule for the next one are shown here

When you first set up Time Machine it copies everything on your Mac. Depending on the type of connection you have for your external drive, this could take several hours. Because of this, it is a good idea to have a hard drive with a USB 3.0 or Thunderbolt connection to make it as fast as possible.

If you stop the initial backup before it has been completed, Time Machine will remember where it has stopped and resume the backup from this point.

...cont'd

Using Time Machine

Once Time Machine has been set up, it can then be used to go back in time to view items in an earlier state. To do this:

Beware

If you have deleted items before the initial set up of Time Machine, these will not be recoverable.

Don't forget

The hard drive must be connected in order to use Time Machine.

Don't forget

The active item that you were viewing before you launched Time Machine is the one that is active in the Time Machine interface. You can select items from within the active window to view their contents.

 Access an item on your Mac and delete it. In this example, the folder **Apple Computing** has been deleted

 Click on the **Time Machine** icon

3 Time Machine displays the selected window in its current state (the Apple Computing folder is deleted). Earlier versions are stacked behind it

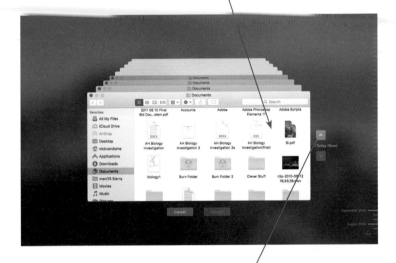

4 Click on the arrows to move through the open items or select a time or date from the scale to the right of the arrows

 Another way to move through Time Machine is to click on the pages behind the first one. This brings the selected item to the front

6 Click on the **Restore** button to restore any items that have been deleted (in this case the Apple Computing folder)

 Restore

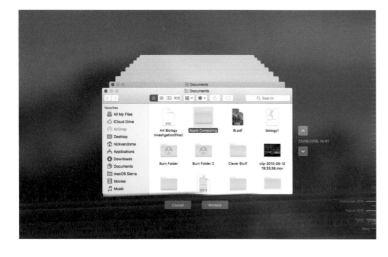

Items are restored from the Time Machine backup disk, i.e. the external hard drive.

7 Click on the **Cancel** button to return to your normal environment

Cancel

8 The deleted folder **Apple Computing** is now restored to its original location

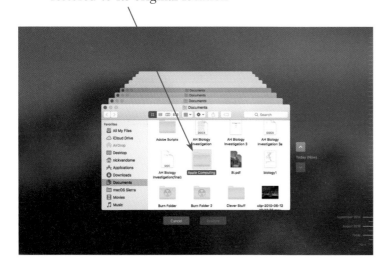

Disk Utility

Disk Utility is a utility app that allows you to perform certain testing and repair functions for macOS. It incorporates a variety of functions and is a good option for both general maintenance, and if your computer is not running as it should.

Each of the functions within Disk Utility can be applied to specific drives and volumes. However, it is not possible to use the macOS start-up disk within Disk Utility as this will be in operation to run the app, and Disk Utility cannot operate on a disk that has apps already running. To use Disk Utility:

Checking disks

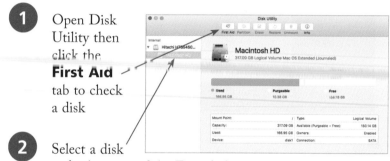

1 Open Disk Utility then click the **First Aid** tab to check a disk

2 Select a disk and select one of the First Aid options

Erasing a disk
To erase all of the data on a disk or a volume:

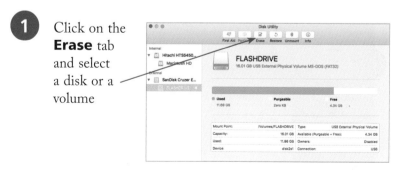

1 Click on the **Erase** tab and select a disk or a volume

2 Click **Erase** to erase the data on the selected disk or volume

---

Disk Utility is located within the **Applications > Utilities** folder.

178

If there is a problem with a disk and macOS can fix it, the **Repair** button will be available. Click on this to enable Disk Utility to repair the problem.

If you erase data from a removable disk, such as a flashdrive, you will not be able to retrieve it.

System Information

This can be used to view how the different hardware and software elements on your Mac are performing. To do this:

 Open the **Utilities** folder and double-click on the **System Information** icon

 Click on the **Hardware** link and click on an item of hardware

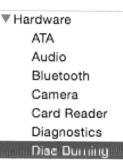

Don't forget

System Information is located within the **Applications** > **Utilities** folder.

Details about the item of hardware, and its performance, are displayed

```
MATSHITA DVD-R  UJ-898:

Firmware Revision:  HE13
Interconnect:       ATAPI
Burn Support:       Yes (Apple Shipping Drive)
Cache:              1024 KB
Reads DVD:          Yes
CD-Write:           -R, -RW
DVD-Write:          -R, -R DL, -RW, +R, +R DL, +RW
Write Strategies:   CD-TAO, CD-SAO, DVD-DAO
Media:              To show the available burn speeds, insert a disc and
                    choose File > Refresh Information
```

Similarly, click on network or software items to view their details

```
Calendar                    8.0

Calendar:

Version:          8.0
Obtained from:    Apple
Last Modified:    16/09/2015, 16:17
Kind:             Intel
64-Bit (Intel):   Yes
Signed by:        Software Signing, Apple Code Signing Certification
                  Authority, Apple Root CA
Location:         /Applications/Calendar.app
```

Activity Monitor

Activity Monitor is a utility app that can be used to view information about how much processing power and memory is being used to run apps. This can be useful to know if certain apps are running slowly or crashing frequently. To use Activity Monitor:

Don't forget

Activity Monitor is located within the **Applications** > **Utilities** folder.

Activity Monitor

 Open the Activity Monitor and click on the **CPU** tab to see how much processor capacity is being used up

System:	1.03%	CPU LOAD	Threads:	719
User:	0.45%		Processes:	187
Idle:	98.51%			

 Click on the **Memory** tab to see how much system memory (RAM) is being used up

MEMORY PRESSURE	Physical Memory:	8.00 GB	App Memory:	1.90 GB
	Memory Used:	2.94 GB	Wired Memory:	1.04 GB
	Cached Files:	1.30 GB	Compressed:	0 bytes
	Swap Used:	0 bytes		

3 Click on the **Disk** tab to see how much space has been taken up on the hard drive

Reads in:	86,144	IO	Data read:	2.65 GB
Writes out:	20,518		Data written:	530.0 MB
Reads in/sec:	0		Data read/sec:	0 bytes
Writes out/sec:	1		Data written/sec:	8.80 KB

Updating Software

Apple periodically releases updates for its software; both its apps and the macOS operating system. All of these are now available through the App Store. To update software:

1 Open **System Preferences** and click on the **App Store** icon

App Store

2 Click here to select options for how you are notified about updates and how they are downloaded

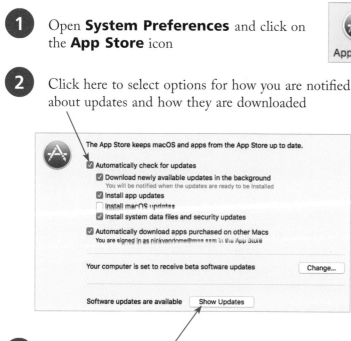

3 To check for updates manually, click on the **Show Updates** button

4 Available updates are shown in the Updates section of the App Store. Click on the **Update** buttons to update. If there are no updates available this will be stated, with the latest updates underneath

Software updates can also be accessed directly from the Apple menu, located on the top Menu bar. If updates are available this is denoted by a red, circled number on the **App Store** link on the Apple menu, or on the App Store app's icon.

Check **On** the **Automatically download apps purchased on other Macs** box if you want to activate this function.

For some software updates, such as those for the macOS itself, you may have to restart your computer for them to take effect.

Gatekeeper

Internet security is an important issue for every computer user; no-one wants their computer to be infected with a virus or malicious software. Historically, Macs have been less prone to attack from viruses than Windows-based machines, but this does not mean Mac users can be complacent. With their increasing popularity there is now more temptation for virus writers to target them. macOS Sierra recognizes this and has taken steps to prevent attacks with the Gatekeeper function. To use this:

Hot tip

To make changes within the General section of the Security & Privacy System Preferences, click on the padlock icon and enter your admin password.

🔒 Click the lock to make changes.

182

1 Open **System Preferences** and click on the **Security & Privacy** icon

Security & Privacy

2 Click on the **General** tab   General

3 Click on one of these buttons to determine which location apps can be downloaded from. You can select from just the Mac App Store, or Mac App Store and identified developers, which gives you added security in terms of apps having been thoroughly checked

Allow apps downloaded from:

◯ App Store

◉ App Store and identified developers

Beware

If a password is not added for logging in to your account, or after sleep, other people could access your account and all of your files.

4 Under the **General** tab there are also options for using a password when you log in to your account, if a password is required after sleep or if the screen saver is activated, showing a message when the screen is locked, or disabling automatic login

A login password has been set for this user   Change Password...

☑ Require password immediately ⬍ after sleep or screen saver begins

☐ Show a message when the screen is locked   Set Lock Message...

☐ Disable automatic login

Privacy

Also within the Security & Privacy System Preferences are options for activating a firewall and privacy settings. To access these:

1 Click on the **Firewall** tab

Firewall

2 Click on the **Turn On Firewall** button to activate this. Click on **Firewall Options...** to change settings for the firewall

3 Click on the **Privacy** tab

Privacy

4 Click on the **Location Services** link and check **On** the **Enable Location Services** option if you want relevant apps to be able to access your location

5 Click on the **Contacts** link and check **On** any relevant apps that are allowed to access your Contacts

6 Click on the **Diagnostics & Usage** link and check **On** the **Send diagnostic & usage data to Apple** if you want to send information to Apple about the performance of your Mac and its apps. This will include any problems, and helps Apple improve its software and apps. This information is collected anonymously and does not identify anyone personally

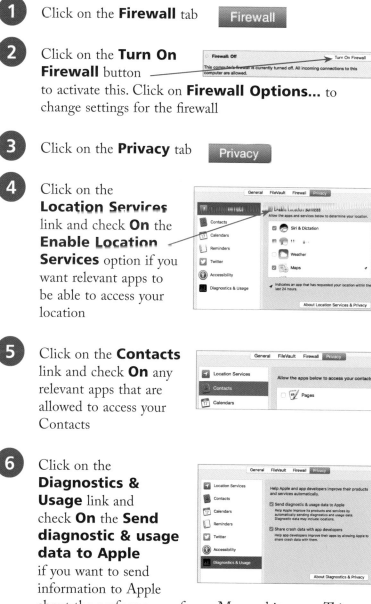

A firewell is an application that aims to stop malicious software from accessing your computer.

macOS Sierra apps are designed to do only what they are supposed to, so that they do not have to interact with other apps if they do not need to. This lessens the possibility of any viruses spreading across your Mac. For instance, only apps that have the ability to use Contacts will ask for permission to do this.

183

Problems with Apps

The simple answer

macOS is something of a rarity in the world of computing software: it claims to be remarkably stable, and it is. However, this is not to say that things do not sometimes go wrong, although this is considerably less frequent than with older Mac operating systems. Sometimes this will be due to problems within particular apps, and on occasions the problems may lie with macOS itself. If this does happen, the first course of action is to restart macOS using the **Apple menu > Restart...** command. If this does not work, or you cannot access the Restart command as the Mac has frozen, try turning off the power to the computer and then starting up again.

Force quitting

If a particular app is not responding, it can be closed down separately without the need to reboot the computer. To do this:

Beware

When there are updates to macOS, these can on rare occasions cause issues with some apps. However, these are usually fixed with subsequent patches and upgrades to macOS.

1 Select **Apple menu > Force Quit...** from the Menu bar

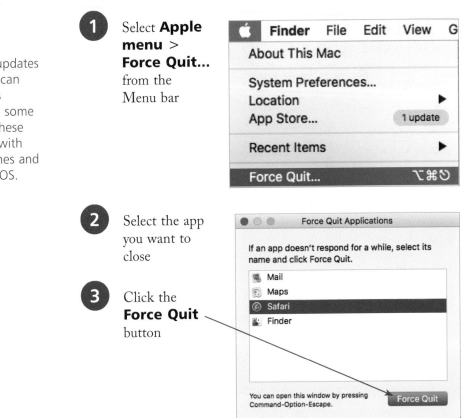

2 Select the app you want to close

3 Click the **Force Quit** button

General Troubleshooting

It is true that things do occasionally go wrong with macOS, although probably with less regularity than with some other operating systems. If something does go wrong, there are a number of areas that you can check and also some steps you can take to ensure that you do not lose any important data if the worst case scenario occurs, and your hard drive packs up completely:

- **Backup**. If everything does go wrong it is essential that you have taken preventative action in the form of making sure that all of your data is backed up and saved. This can be done with either the Time Machine app or by backing up manually by copying data to a CD or DVD. Some content is also automatically backed up if you have iCloud activated.

- **Reboot**. One traditional reply by IT helpdesks is to reboot, i.e. turn off the computer and turn it back on again and hope that the problem has resolved itself. In a lot of cases this simple operation does the trick, but it is not always a viable solution for major problems.

- **Check cables**. If the problem appears to be with a network connection or an externally connected device, check that all cables are connected properly and have not become loose. If possible, make sure that all cables are tucked away so that they cannot be inadvertently pulled out.

- **Check network settings**. If your network or internet connections are not working, check the network settings in System Preferences. Sometimes when you make a change to one item, this can have an adverse effect on one of these settings. (If possible, lock the settings once you have applied them by clicking on the padlock icon in the Network preferences window.)

- **Check for viruses**. If your computer is infected with a virus this could affect the efficient running of the machine. Luckily, this is less of a problem for Macs as virus writers tend to concentrate their efforts towards Windows-based machines. However, this is changing as Macs become more popular, and there are plenty of Mac viruses out there. So make sure your computer is protected by an app such as Norton AntiVirus which is available from **www.norton.com**

Don't forget

In extreme cases, you will not be able to reboot your computer normally. If this happens, you will have to pull out the power cable and re-attach it. You will then be able to reboot, although the computer may want to check its hard drive to make sure that everything is in working order.

...cont'd

Beware

If you are having problems opening a document that you have been sent from a trusted source, contact them to make sure that the document has not been locked with a password. If you receive documents from someone you do not know, such as by email, do not open them as they may contain viruses or malware.

Don't forget

Within the Screen Saver section is a button for **Hot Corners**. Click on this to access options for specifying what happens when the cursor is pointed over the four corners of the screen. This includes accessing the Notification Center, the Launchpad or putting the Mac display to Sleep.

- **Check Start-up items**. If you have set certain items to start automatically when your computer is turned on, this could cause certain conflicts within your machine. If this is the case, disable the items from launching during the booting up of the computer. This can be done within the Users & Groups section of System Preferences by clicking on the **Login Items** tab, selecting the relevant item and pressing the minus button.

- **Check permissions**. If you or other users are having problems opening items, this could be because of the permissions that are set. To check these, select the item in the Finder, click on the **File** button on the top Menu bar and select **Get Info**. In the **Sharing & Permissions** section of the Info window you will be able to set the relevant permissions to allow other users, or yourself, to read, write or have no access.

Click here to view Permissions settings

- **Eject external devices**. Sometimes external devices, such as flashdrives, can become temperamental and refuse to eject the disks within them, or even not show up on the Desktop or in the Finder at all. If this happens, you can try to eject the disk by pressing the mouse button when the Mac chimes are heard during the booting up process.

- **Turn off your screen saver**. Screen savers can sometimes cause conflicts within your computer, particularly if they have been downloaded from an unreliable source. If this happens, change the screen saver within the **Screen Saver** tab in the **Desktop & Screen Saver** preference of the System Preferences, or disable it altogether.

Index

A

About Your Mac   12-16
   Display information   13
   Memory information   14
   Overview   13
   Service   15
   Storage information   14
   Support   15
Accessibility   23-24
Activity Monitor   128, 180
Address book.   *See* Contacts
AirDrop   169
AirPort   167
AirPort Utility   128
Apple ID   41, 105, 142, 153
Apple menu   10
Apple Music   154-155
   Subscription   154
AppleScript   128
Apple Watch
   For unlocking a Mac   26
Apps
   Automator   104
   Calculator   104
   Calendar   104
   Chess   104
   Contacts   104
   Dashboard   104
   Dictionary   104
   Downloading   106-107
   DVD Player   104
   FaceTime   104
   Finding   108-109
   Font Book   104
   Force quitting   184
   GarageBand   104
   iBooks   104
   iMovie   104
   iPhoto   104
   iTunes   104
   Keynote   104
   macOS apps   104
   Mail   104
   Managing   110
   Maps   104
   Messages   104
   Mission Control   104
   Notes   104
   Numbers   104
   Pages   104
   Photo Booth   104
   Photos   104
   Preview   104
   Purchased   110
   QuickTime Player   104
   Reminders   104
   Safari   104
   Searching for   108
   TextEdit   104
   Time Machine   104
   Updating   110
     Automatically   110
App Store   105
   Accessing   105
   Categories   108-109
   Featured   108
   Top Charts   109
   Top Free   108
   Top Paid   108
   Using with an Apple ID   105
Audio MIDI Setup   128
Automator   104

B

Background wallpaper   16, 38
Backing up
   With iCloud   40
   With Time Machine   174-175
Bluetooth File Exchange   128
Books.   *See* iBooks
Boot Camp Assistant   128
   For using Windows   100

C

Calendar   114-115
   Adding Events   115
   Continuous scrolling   114
   Finding locations   115
Changing overall appearance   16
Chess   104
Color adjustments. *See* Photos app: Editing photos
ColorSync   128
Command Key   69

Console   128
Contacts   112-113
  Contact information
    Adding   112
  Groups
    Creating   113
Continuity   44-45
Copy and paste   67
Copying
  By dragging   67
Covers   62

D

Desktop   10, 52
  Showing   91
Desktop items   52
Dictation   25
Dictionary   104
DigitalColor Meter   129
Disk Utility   129, 178
  Checking disks   178
  Erasing a disk   178
Dock   28-36
  Adding items   35
  Genie effect   31
  Keep in Dock option   35
  Magnification   31
  Menus   34
  Overview   28
  Positioning   30
  Preferences   30-31
  Quit option   34
  Removing items   36
  Removing open apps   36
  Resizing manually   31
  Show In Finder option   34
  Stacking items   32-33
Drop Box   171-172
  Accessing   172
Dropbox app   171
DVDs
  Creating   152

E

eBooks.   See iBooks
Effects.   See Photos app: Editing photos
Ejecting items   53, 186

Email   140-141
Enhancing photos. See Photos app: Editing photos
Ethernet   166-168
Exposé   96
External devices
  Ejecting   186

F

Facebook   39, 120
FaceTime   144
Family Sharing   46-51
  Finding lost family devices   51
  Setting up   46-47
  Sharing calendars   50
  Sharing music, apps and books   48-49
  Using   48-49
Fast user switching   161
Finder   56-67
  Actions button   56, 76
  All My Files   57
  Applications   58
  Arrangement button   77
  Back button   59
  Documents   58
  Folders   57-58, 74-75
  Home folder   58
  Overview   56
  Search   66
  Sharing from   77
  Sidebar   65
    Adding items to   65
  Tabs   70-71
  Tags   72-73, 76
  Toolbar
    Customizing   64
  Views   59-64
    Column view   61
    Icon view   60
    List view   61-62
Finder search   17
Finding things with Finder   66
Flickr   77
Flyover.   See Maps: Flyover Tour
Folders
  Burnable   75
  Creating new   58, 68
  Deleting   58
  Spring-loaded   74
Force quitting   184
Force Touch   80
Full screen apps   102-103

G

GarageBand   104, 152
Gatekeeper   182
Google   66
Grab   129
Grapher   129
Guest users   171-172

H

Handoff   45
  Support   12
Haptic feedback   80
Hotspot   133

I

iBooks   155-156
  Library   156
  Previewing titles   155
  Toolbars for books   156
iCloud   40-44
  Keychain   43
  Online account   41
  Setting up   41
  Storage   40
iCloud Drive   42-43
  Desktop & Documents Folders   42
iMac with Retina Display   84
iMessages   142
  Adding photos and videos 143
  Audio messages   143
iMovie   104, 152
Internet
  Getting connected   132-133, 185
Internet Accounts
  Adding   135
Internet Service Provider 132
iOS
  For messaging   142
iPhone   144
iPhoto   104, 146
iTunes   104, 152-154
  Purchasing music   153
iTunes Store   153
iWork   104

K

Keychain   43
Keychain Access   129
Keynote   43

L

Labeling items   76
LAN (Local Area Network)   166
Launchpad   100-101
LinkedIn   39
Location Services   122, 183
Lock screen   26

M

macOS Sierra
  About   8
  Compatible Mac computers 9
  From the App Store   9
  Installing   9
  Working environment   10-11
macOS Utilities   128-129
Magic Mouse   80
  Gestures   92-94
Magic Trackpad   80
Mail   104, 140-141
Maps   122-125
  Finding locations   123
  Flyover Tour   123
  Getting directions   124
  Map view   123
  Satellite view   123
  Transit directions   125
  Transit view   123
  Viewing   122
Menus   78
  Apple menu   78
  Edit menu   78
  File menu   78
  Finder menu   78
  Go   78
  Help   78
  View   78
  Window   78

Messages	104, 142
Deleting a conversation	143
Emojis	142
iMessages	142
SMS messages	142-143
Tapback	143
Text messages	142-143
Migration Assistant	129
Mission Control	97-98
Moving between full screen apps	90
Moving between pages	90
Multiple displays	38
Multiple users	
Adding users	158-159
Deleting users	160
Fast user switching	161
Multi-Touch Gestures	80, 95-96
Multi-Touch Preferences	95
More Gestures	96
Point & Click	96
Scroll & Zoom	96
Music	
Importing	152

N

Navigating	80
Magic Mouse gestures	92-94
Multi-Touch preferences	95-96
Trackpad gestures	84-91, 95-96
Network	
File sharing	
Drop Box	172
Guest users	171-172
Setting up	169
Networking	
AirPort base station	167
AirPort Express	167
Airport Extreme	167
Airport network	167
Connecting to a network	170
Ethernet cable	166
Ethernet network	167
File sharing	169-172
Hub	166
IEEE 802.11 standards	167
Network card	166
Network settings	168
Overview	166-167
Router	
Wireless	166
Switch	166

Wi-Fi	167
Wireless network	167
Network Interface Card	166
Notes	116-117
Adding check buttons	117
Adding photos and videos	117
Attachments Browser	117
Formatting	117
With iCloud	116
Notification Center	120-121
Notifications	120-121
Alerts	121
Viewing	121
Numbers	43

O

Online security	163
Optimized Storage	14
Empty Trash automatically	14
Reduce clutter	14
Removing movies and TV shows	14
Store in iCloud	14
Option buttons	11

P

Pages	43
Parental controls	162-164
Enable	162
Stores controls	163
Time controls	164
Web controls	163
Password	
For logging in	26
PDF	126
Creating documents	130
Personal Hotspot	133
Phone call forwarding	144
Photos app	
Editing photos	149
Importing photos	147
Memories	150-151
Using with iCloud	146
Viewing photos	147-148
Playing music.	See iTunes
Portable Document Format.	See PDF
Preview	126
Printing	127

Privacy		183
Programs (apps)		
Force quitting		184

Q

Quick Look	63
QuickTime Player	104
Quitting apps	184

R

Radio stations	
Beats 1	154
With Apple Music	154
RAM	100
Reading List	139
Reminders	118-119
Removable disks	52
Resolution	
Changing	22
Screen	22
Resuming	26, 54

S

Safari	104, 134-139
Bookmarks	
Adding	138
Favorites page	134
Overview	134
Reader	139
Share button	139
Shared Links	135
Sidebar	134-135
Tabbed browsing	136
Top Sites	136-137
Script Editor	129
Screen saver	16, 186
Scroll bars	81
Scrolling	
Up and down	86-87
Searching for items	17
Searching with Finder	66
Searching the internet	134

Selecting	
By clicking	69-70
By dragging	69
Select All	69
Sharing	117
From Finder	77
From Maps	124
From Notes	117
From Safari	139
Sharing content to Notes	117
Short Message Service.	*See* SMS messages
Shutting down	26
Siri	17-21
Drag and drop results	20
Multitasking	20
Pinning results	21
Searching for documents	19
Search options	19
Setting up	18
Sleep mode	26
SMS messages	142
Social networking	
Linking to accounts	39, 135
Software updates	121, 181
Spaces	98
Deleting	98
Split View	82-83
Spotlight search	17
Storage	
Optimizing	14
SuperDrive	38
System Information	179
System Preferences	38-39
About	16
Hardware	38
CDs & DVDs	38
Displays	38
Energy Saver	38
Keyboard	38
Mouse	38
Printers & Scanners	38
Sound	39
Startup Disk	39
Trackpad	38
Internet & Wireless	39
App Store	39
Bluetooth	39
Extensions	39
iCloud	39
Internet Accounts	39
Network	39
Sharing	39
Personal	38
Dictation	38
Desktop & Screen Saver	38

Dock	38
General	38
Language & Region	38
Mission Control	38
Notifications	38
Security & Privacy	38
Spotlight	38
System	39
Accessibility	39
Date & Time	39
Parental Controls	39
Siri	39
Time Machine	39
Users & Groups	39

T

Tab bar	
In macOS apps	70
Tabbed browsing	136
Tabs.	See Finder: Tabs
Tags.	See Finder: Tags
Terminal	129
TextEdit	104
Text forwarding	143
Time Machine	104, 174-177
Setting up	174
Using	176
Trackpad	80-81, 84-91, 95-96
Trash	37, 53
Troubleshooting	
Backing up	185
Cables	185
External devices	186
Network settings	185
Overview	185
Permissions	186
Rebooting	185
Screen savers	186
Start-up items	186
Viruses	185
Twitter	39, 77, 120

U

Universal Clipboard	67
UNIX	8
User accounts	
Deleting users	160

Fast user switching	161
Utilities	128-129
Activity Monitor	128
AirPort Utility	128
Audio MIDI Setup	128
Bluetooth File Exchange	128
Boot Camp Assistant	128
ColorSync Utility	128
Console	128
DigitalColor Meter	129
Disk Utility	129
Grab	129
Grapher	129
Keychain Access	129
Migration Assistant	129
Script Editor	129
System Information	129
Terminal	129
VoiceOver Utility	129

V

Viewing files without opening	63
Viewing PDFs with Preview	126
Viewing photos.	See Photos app: Viewing photos
Viruses	185
In email	186
VoiceOver	23
VoiceOver Utility	129

W

Window buttons	11
Windows on a Mac	100, 128
Wireless network	166-167

Y

YouTube	104

Z

Zooming in and out	88-89